KETO MEAL PREP COOKBOOK

Keto Meal Prep Cookbook

Complete Meal Prep Cookbook for the Ketogenic Diet; 30 Day Meal Planner with Full Nutrition Facts Including Net Carbs

By: Jane Easton

Legal Notice

Contents

How I 'Went Keto' 15

Introduction to the Ketogenic Meal Prep Cookbook 18

    A quick overview of the Ketogenic Diet...19

    Why a new energy source is crucial for a healthy body 21

    The health benefits of the Ketogenic Diet....................................22

    Which foods should and should not be eaten on the Ketogenic Diet? 23

    The best ways to cook food on the Ketogenic Diet 26

DAY-1 BREAKFAST 29

Delicious Mexican Frittata.. 29

DAY-1 LUNCH 30

Tasty Chicken Guacamole Salad 30

DAY-1 DINNER 31

Flavorful Chicken Piccata.. 31

DAY-2 BREAKFAST 32

Healthy Egg Breakfast Muffins 32

DAY-2 LUNCH 33

Creamy Cheesy Cauliflower Mash 33

DAY-2 DINNER 34

Cauliflower Cheese Casserole 34

DAY-3 BREAKFAST 36

Jalapeno Muffins.. 36

DAY-3 LUNCH.. 37

Bacon Avocado Chicken Salad...37

DAY-3 DINNER 38

Perfect Bacon Chicken..38

DAY-4 BREAKFAST 39

Easy Breakfast Bowl..39

DAY-4 LUNCH 40

Creamy Egg Salad...40

DAY-4 DINNER 41

Quick Cherry Tomato Frittata...41

DAY-5 BREAKFAST 42

Egg Breakfast Casserole 42

DAY-5 LUNCH 43

Chicken Basil Salad 43

DAY-5DINNER 44

Smoked Paprika Chicken 44

DAY-6 BREAKFAST 45

Almond Blueberry Muffins...45

DAY-6 LUNCH 46

Mayo Shrimp Cilantro Salad 46

DAY-6 DINNER 47

Simple Coconut Shrimp..47

DAY-7 BREAKFAST 48

Cheddar Broccoli Bread..48

DAY-7 LUNCH 49

Flavorful Tuna Salad...49

DAY-7 DINNER 50

Tuna Egg Bake 50

DAY-8 BREAKFAST 52

Delicious Ricotta Omelet 52

DAY-8 LUNCH 53

Flavorful Citrusy Shrimp 53

DAY-8 DINNER 54

Simple Old Bay Seasoned Shrimp 54

DAY-9 BREAKFAST 55

Olive Bacon Quiche 55

DAY-9 LUNCH 57

Easy Cabbage Noodles 57

DAY-9 DINNER 58

Cauliflower Cheese Casserole 58

DAY-10 BREAKFAST 59

Coconut Waffles 59

DAY-10 LUNCH 60

Curried Chicken Salad 60

DAY-10 DINNER 61

Cheese Broccoli Soup 61

DAY-11 BREAKFAST 62

Easy Egg Loaf 62

DAY-11 LUNCH 63

Almond Chicken Salad 63

DAY-11 DINNER 64

Shrimp Mushroom Soup 64

DAY-12 BREAKFAST 65

Delicious Breakfast Cookies 65

DAY-12 LUNCH 66

Cucumber Tuna Salad 66

DAY-12 DINNER 67

Delicious Ranch Chicken 67

DAY-13 BREAKFAST 68

Bacon Cheese Bread 68

DAY-13 LUNCH 69

Chili Garlic Shrimp 69

DAY-13 DINNER 70

Pesto Cheese Salmon 70

DAY-14 BREAKFAST 71

Coconut Chia Pudding 71

DAY-14 LUNCH 72

Avocado Bacon Soup 72

DAY-14 DINNER 73

Lemon Parmesan Salmon 73

DAY-15 BREAKFAST 74

Spinach Bacon Frittata 74

DAY-15 LUNCH 75

Italian Pepperoni Avocado Salad 75

DAY-15 DINNER 76

Garlic Onion Pork Tenderloin 76

DAY-16 BREAKFAST 77

Healthy Coconut Porridge 77

DAY-16 LUNCH 78

Cilantro Shrimp Avocado Salad 78

DAY-16 DINNER 79

Lemon Garlic Chicken 79

DAY-17 BREAKFAST 80

Bacon Avocado Quiche 80

DAY-17 LUNCH 81

Perfect Geek Salad 81

DAY-17 DINNER 82

Zucchini Cheese Casserole 82

DAY-18 BREAKFAST 83

Healthy Spinach Quiche 83

DAY-18 LUNCH 84

Healthy Mediterranean Salad 84

DAY-18 DINNER 85

Tasty Pumpkin Spiced Soup 85

DAY-19 BREAKFAST 86

Almond Pumpkin Pancake 86

DAY-19 LUNCH 87

Refreshing Creamy Cucumber Salad 87

DAY-19 DINNER 88

Herb Chicken 88

DAY-20 BREAKFAST 89

Blueberry Almond Coconut Flour Casserole.. 89

DAY-20 LUNCH.. 90

Delicious Zucchini Soup.. 90

DAY-20 DINNER 91

Zucchini Cheese Gratin... 91

DAY-21 BREAKFAST 92

Creamy Egg Scrambled 92

DAY-21 LUNCH.. 93

Easy Chicken Fajitas... 93

DAY-21 DINNER 94

Zucchini Noodles.. 94

DAY-22 BREAKFAST 95

Cauliflower Cheese Bread 95

DAY-22 LUNCH.. 96

Mayo Cabbage Coleslaw 96

DAY-22 DINNER 97

Cauliflower Cheese Gratin.. 97

DAY-23 BREAKFAST 98

Herb Cauliflower Bread.. 98

DAY-23 LUNCH.. 99

Cabbage Dill Cucumber Salad.. 99

DAY-23 DINNER 100

Cheese Cauliflower Rice 100

DAY-24 BREAKFAST 101

Vanilla protein Muffins... 101

DAY-24 LUNCH 102

Healthy Coconut Spinach Soup 102

DAY-24 DINNER 103

Baked Broccoli.. 103

DAY-25 BREAKFAST 104

Coconut Kale Muffins... 104

DAY-25 LUNCH 105

Garlic Herb Baked Mushrooms 105

DAY-25 DINNER 106

Parmesan Spinach Pie 106

DAY-26 BREAKFAST 108

Spicy & Creamy Egg Scrambled 108

DAY-26 LUNCH 109

Creamy Cauliflower Broccoli Mashed 109

DAY-26 DINNER 110

Almond Jalapeno Pizza... 110

DAY-27 BREAKFAST 111

Cinnamon Cream Egg Scrambled... 111

DAY-27 LUNCH 112

Paprika Egg Cucumber Salad 112

DAY-27 DINNER 113

Spinach Casserole 113

DAY-28 BREAKFAST 115

Flavorful Cheese Quiche... 115

DAY-28 LUNCH 116

Easy Caesar Salad 116

DAY-28 DINNER 117

Cheese Chicken Casserole 117

DAY-29 BREAKFAST 118

Tasty Cauliflower Frittata 118

DAY-29 LUNCH 119

Flavors Squash Soup 119

DAY-29 DINNER 120

Spicy Chicken Curry 120

DAY-30 BREAKFAST 121

Mushroom Asparagus Frittata 121

DAY-30 LUNCH 122

Simple Broccoli Omelet 122

DAY-30 DINNER 123

Meatloaf 123

References and resources 124

THE "DIRTY DOZEN" AND "CLEAN 15" 126

THE DIRTY DOZEN 126

THE CLEAN 15 126

Measurement Conversion Tables 127

Final Note from the Author 128

Alphabetical Recipe Index 130

14

How I 'Went Keto'

I've had a very difficult time in my life trying to adapt to a diet that was both easy to stick to and also easy to plan for. With three children and a full-time job, trying to lose weight and stay healthy at the same time is really not something that comes easily to me. However, after quite a bit of research, I was finally able to discover the Ketogenic Diet and to full introduce and incorporate it into my life and even my family's life. Although I certainly don't make my family members follow the diet as precisely as I do, I am really glad that they have shown a true interest in it and that they were also able to reap the health and weight loss benefits from this way of eating.

One of my favorite things about this diet is the fact that all of the ingredients are wholefoods, and that both sugar and salt are reduced to their minimum levels of use. One of the main reasons why I experienced so many health problems was precisely because I was eating too much sugar and salt, as well as too many processed foods, which resulted in bloating, weight gain, and an increase in blood pressure. I hadn't immediately realized that food would be able to help me solve this problem, but I am proud to say that after only a few weeks on the Ketogenic Diet, I noticed a serious change in my health and the way that I was feeling about my body overall. I love that I can prepare easy recipes that fit the household budget, and that can also be made days in advance so that I don't have to worry about them. I can easily plan my meals throughout the week, and I also make sure to cook in larger quantities so that I can include my family into this way of eating.

When I recall how difficult it was for me to eat healthily and to take care of myself, I am a little sad that I didn't discover the Ketogenic Diet earlier. However, I am delighted that I was able to find it now and that my body has adapted to this diet so easily. I have noticed serious changed such as weight loss, a spike in my energy levels, and also a much better set of blood tests when I went for my annual checkup.

I have been on the Ketogenic Diet for about two years now, and I would honestly never go back to my old ways of eating ever again. I hope that I can help to introduce this diet to more people around the world, and I also hope that they will be able to notice all of the health changes that come with this way of eating. It is almost the perfect diet for this day and age, and it forces you to make sure that everything that you put into your body comes from wholefoods, which is crucial for health and happiness.

With love,

Jane Easton

Introduction to the Ketogenic Meal Prep Cookbook

The Ketogenic Diet is not a new way of eating in the world, but it is certainly a style of eating that has rightfully attracted a lot of attention from people who knew very little about it before. Considering how busy our current lifestyles are at the moment, it is understandable that people are finding it very difficult to match eating, fitness, stress-balance, and their family lives in a perfect mix. In fact, it is almost impossible to create an atmosphere where all of these things come together in the perfect way. Because so many people have such a difficult time prepping their everyday lives, one of the first things that goes out the window when it comes to balance is food.

The kind of food that we eat in the modern world revolves around things that are super quick to make, full of intense flavors, such as salt and sugar, and also full of additive and preservatives, so that they can last us a long time and we won't have to go grocery shopping often. Although it is certainly understandable that people are doing everything they can to balance their lives with their budget, when we ruin the way that we eat and the way that we nourish our bodies, we essential ruin the most important thing on a daily basis.

A body that has not been treated properly will lack energy, cause anxiety and depression, and it will also not be able to focus for long periods of time, which mean that our work lives will also have to suffer as a result.

This is not good, and in the long run, could be the cause of higher levels of anxiety in people and a loss of hope for a healthier life with less weight. However, the Ketogenic Diet is a way of eating that can truly help people overcome their poor eating habits, and could also show them a new style of living where individuals can form their own eating schedules, while still sticking to a diet that is easy to manage and easy to prepare.

A quick overview of the Ketogenic Diet

Before we move on to discuss how you can prepare for the Ketogenic Diet, we must first discuss what this diet actually is, what makes it so special, and which parts of this way of eating are the most crucial ones when it comes to living a healthier lifestyle. The diet itself is, luckily, not difficult to understand, but the more you know about it, the easier it will be for you to adapt and to get the most out of this style of eating.

The Ketogenic Diet is a diet that is comprised of wholefoods and high fat. It first appeared as a diet that was found to be able to help children with epilepsy problems, and was then extended to the wider public because there were a number of other health benefits that were discovered along the way. For the wider public, it is the chemistry behind the diet that makes it so useful for the wider masses, and why it is so effective when it comes to weight loss.

The chemistry behind this diet has to do with carbohydrates and energy sources of our bodies, which not only dictate our actual energy levels, but they are also dictate our weight, mood, and other health issues. Namely, it is often well-known to people that carbohydrates are our main source of energy. Whenever your body needs energy to do anything, it will always go to your carbohydrate sources first, and will use them all up entirely before it even tries to move on to another energy source. The reason why the body really loves carbs as energy is because carbs are super easy to break down and the use. It is very little effort from your body to select a group of carbs and create a burst of energy. Carbs are not bad for you though! Every aspect of food has its own positive and negative takes on the human body, but the thing that is important is to stick to the sources that are healthies and that will bring your body the best results.

However, there is a problem when it comes to carbohydrates. The problem is that we usually takes these carbs from food sources that are really not healthy for our bodies at all. This is usually through fast food, drinks, and desserts. Ever notice that it is precisely these foods that we so often crave? Some of the reasons for this are because our brain craves an instant source of happiness to make us happier faster, but the other side of the truth is precisely the source of energy that comes from carbohydrates. However, the other problem is the fact that our usual day jobs are almost always sedentary. We don't move nearly as much as people used to move before, which means that we are actually gaining weight much faster than previous generations. This is obviously very bad for our health, which is why we need to make a change in our life that will not ruin the health of our bodies.

The way to deal with this is with the help of the Ketogenic Diet. This diet is based on entirely wholefoods, especially those that are in season, and it is also based on the kind of diet that is truly high in fats. The reason why this is such good news for your body is because wholefoods are all we have left to make sure that we are feeding our bodies with the nutrients and the minerals that will actually be able to make us healthier overall. The great thing about the Ketogenic Diet is that the wholefoods that you choose to make your food from are always encouraged to be those that are in season. This is great for a number of reasons. One of those reasons is the fact that foods that are in season are cheaper than those that are imported from far places around the world, and which obviously cost more to arrive to their destination. This is also not good because these foods often have dangerous preservatives in order to make them last longer, but which in turn have negative effects on our bodies. Also, it is much easier to prepare your meals with wholefoods that are easy for you to purchase, and especially those that you can purchase from your local wholefoods producers, which also ensures that you are helping smaller agricultural businesses to succeed. Therefore, there are many positive reasons why the Ketogenic Diet is great both for the individual and for their environment.

WHY A NEW ENERGY SOURCE IS CRUCIAL FOR A HEALTHY BODY

Our bodies really love to stay in a situation that is super predictable. This is because our bodies don't like to be caught in surprise, because this means that the body needs to find a new way to manage itself and to deal with the environment. Whenever something new happens, our body is certainly great at adapting to the new situation, but it is safe to say that it is definitely not something that it wants to do. However, the thing that few people are aware of is that our body has a number of energy sources that it can use to make sure that everything is constantly in order. We already mentioned that carbs are the body's favorite source of energy, but the second favorite source of energy that our body can use is our own fat. However, the body will not try to use any of the fat storages that we have until it has completely used up all of the available carbs. This is because carbs are both easy to store and easy to burn, and also because we rarely reach a point in our lives where we will naturally use up all of the carbs inside of our system and finally make our body shift to using fat. This is because of the problem of modern day life that we have previously mentioned, where we live lives where we don't really use up a lot of energy, which means that our body will actually store the remaining carbs in our system and turn them into additional fat, which is the thing that most frequently causes weight gain. So how do we make our bodies switch to another source of energy?

Well, the most logical way to do this is to restrict the body from the source of energy that it is so used to, which are carbs. When we reduce the amount of carbs that we eat, it means that the body will burn them much faster than it was used to burning them before, which means that it will have no choice but to switch to fat as a new source of energy. Note though that this is not something that happens instantly. Depending on the kind of lifestyle that you were leading prior to you decision to switch to a Ketogenic Diet, it could take anywhere between two days and four days for the entire Ketogenic effect to take place. This is where patience really comes in as the most important source of motivation during this initial period of transition onto this style of eating. Also, some of the most frequent problems that people experience are headaches and sudden cravings. This is precisely because the body is doing everything it can to go back to the old way of eating, because it really doesn't want to deal with the complex process that is the breakdown of fatty acids as energy sources, but if you are able to push through this short period at the beginning, the body will have no other choice but to switch to a new energy source.

After a few days have passed and all of the carbohydrate sources have been used up, the body will switch t breaking down fatty acids into an energy source. The body needs the help of the liver in order to do this properly, but once this process had been completed, the source of energy that comes from fats is a powerful, and stable one. It is also the main reason why so many people report serious weight loss when they transfer to the Ketogenic Diet, and if they keep it up, the weight loss will be more and more visible and continuous for as long as the body has any extra weight to lose. But this isn't the only reason why the Ketogenic Diet is such a great thing overall for the entire body.

THE HEALTH BENEFITS OF THE KETOGENIC DIET

Weight loss is of course a great benefit of a healthy diet, and it has nothing to do with the traditional notions of beauty. The reason why weight loss is important is because all extra weight of the body has a negative effect on the spine and the joints of the body. It makes it very difficult for us to move properly and to live our lives on a daily basis. The less weight that our body has to deal with, the easier it is to live our daily lives. Also, the toxins that come with bad food choices also affect our minds and the way that our brains work. Our brains needs to be fed with healthy foods if they are to work properly and to stay healthy for a long time. Likewise, the introduction of wholefoods also means that our body will easily be able to get rid of cholesterol and also of any sign of diabetes, because there will not be any negative food sources that will cause this kind of trouble for our bodies. There are also numerous other health benefits such as eye health, hair, nail and skin health, and so much more.

The longer that the Ketogenic Diet is applied, the more time the body will have to regenerate itself into a better version of itself, and in turn it will make our lives easier and more pleasurable. Although the positive effects can certainly be noticed even in the first week of switching to a Ketogenic Diet, this does not mean that a single week is enough to change years of bad eating habits and other bad habits that may have been done to the body. As an individual, you still need to make sure that you continue to have your annual checkups with your doctor, and that you continue to have a variety of exercise sources so that your body can truly be in the best shape that it can possible be. We mention this because we don't want to provide a feeling where the change of diet alone will change everything negative that was done for years in the past. However, it is well-known that food certainly is a truly important factor when it comes to the health of the body and it needs to be taken seriously.

WHICH FOODS SHOULD AND SHOULD NOT BE EATEN ON THE KETOGENIC DIET?

In order to create the Ketogenic effect that is so important for this diet, the kind of food that will be eaten needs to be prepared and understood properly. Yes, there will be many foods that we are used to that need to be instantly eliminated from this diet, but it is truly all for the best in the long run. A few days of cravings are well worth the effort when you think of all the great benefits that will come with this new way of eating. Therefore, in order to make sure that everything is correctly understood about the Ketogenic Diet, here is an in-depth look at all the foods that should and should not be eaten and why.

Drink plenty of water

Although some people may think it almost annoying at this point how often they are told to drink water, there is a very important reason why this advice is crucial both in everyday life, but also when it comes to any change that you are making in your diet. It is also extremely important when it comes to transitioning onto the Ketogenic Diet, because your body will need a constant source of water to make sure that it can deal with all of the changes that are about to happen to it. Water is extremely important when it comes to digestion, when it comes to hydrating the human brain and making sure that it will work properly, and also when it comes to making sure that the body will be flushing out all do the toxins that really should no longer be part of it. This means that a good source of water will actually make the Ketogenic Diet more effective, it will help the body to get rid of the bad carbs faster, and it will also reduce the chance of those craving headaches from happening, which is something that so many people have to deal with. To do this properly, make sure that there is always a glass of water near you and try to sip on water continuously. Do not force yourself to drink huge amounts of water at a single time. Instead, make it a natural transition and one where your body will be continuously hydrated at all times.

No sugar, processed foods, grains, or fruit

These are the ingredients that have the highest levels of carbohydrates in them, and they are the main reason why a Ketogenic effect where the body switches to fat as a source of energy is slowed down. When these foods are eliminated, the body will be stopped from having its most favorite source of energy, and it will have to switch to fatty acids one way or another. This means that you must eliminate all processes foods, all desserts, snacks, and sugar, all grains, and all fruit for the time being. This is to make sure that the initial stages of the ketosis are enabled as soon as possible, so that the body can start to feel the benefits oft this diet quickly. Now, you might be thinking that fruit is in fact a healthy ingredient, so why would it be excluded from this diet? Fruit has a very high level of carbs as part of its ingredients, which means that even a single fruit can really ruin all of the previous hard work that has been made to switch to ketosis. Now, because wholefood fruit does in fact have positive effects on the human body, controlled amounts of fruit can later be reintroduced into the diet. However, this is done after the body has already taken up most of the healthy benefits of this diet and at a time when it can afford to have a few fruits every now and them. However, the processed foods should continue to be avoided at all times, because they truly have no benefit for the human body and should not be consumed at any time. For those people who find themselves continue to crave some fast foods or dessert options, there are plenty of Ketogenic versions of these recipes that can be made, which will ensure that you can treat yourself every now and then without disrupting your body.

A lot of protein – from all sources

All protein sources are great for the Ketogenic Diet because they all have healthy sources of fat which will continue to be a great source of energy during this lifestyle change. Of course, this includes the fact that the source of protein need to be ones of the highest quality possible, and prepared in organic ways. Some of the best sources of protein to take inspiration from are pork, poultry, beef, fish, eggs, and seafood. Basically, any source of protein that you really enjoy eating is a great choice. When it comes to the fat content that comes from these ingredients, although you can take away any extra fat that you don't want to include in your recipe, remember that it is this far that will really help your body in the long run. One other important thing to remember is that you need to make sure that you are familiar with where your protein sources are actually coming from. If possible, choose organic options from animals that have lived an organic life on a farm, and not animals that have been force fed to grow larger at a faster rate. Poor sources of protein will have very negative effects on your body and will cause the inclusion of toxins in your diet, which remember are the things that we really want to get rid of.

Plenty of vegetables – especially leafy greens

Vegetables are extremely important for the Ketogenic Diet because they are an important source of vitamins and minerals that will help the body to run properly and to have the right energy levels that you need for your daily tasks. The best choices are spinach, kale, beans, radishes, spring onions, herbs, and beans. These are the ingredients that have the lowest number of carbs in them, or in some cases none at all. However, this does not mean that other sources of vegetables should be avoided, even if they have a higher levels of carbs. This includes vegetables such as carrots, sweet potatoes, potatoes, and red onions. They may have a higher levels of carbs in them, but it is certainly not enough to ruin the ketosis that you are aiming for, and they should be eaten in moderation. Your body still needs the energy source that it needs to run properly. As long as your energy sources are wholefoods, your body will find a way to make itself feel better.

THE BEST WAYS TO COOK FOOD ON THE KETOGENIC DIET

Now that you know the kinds of foods that are allowed and not allowed on the Ketogenic Diet, it is a good idea to go over some of the ways that these foods can be prepared. It will help you to choose the cooking styles that are most suitable for your lifestyle and your food taste, and it will also ensure that you have all the information that you need to make sure that you are preparing your food in the best way possible.

Whenever possible, do not fry your food in large amount of oil. Yes, oil may technically be classified as fat, but it is not necessarily a healthy source of fat, especially not oil that is brought to very high temperatures. Instead, consider baking your food, boiling it, or cooking it in a hot pot or an air cooker. All of these coking methods will ensure that your food will retain as many of its nutritional properties that it can possibly retain, which is of course important for keeping your body healthy. Also, avoid ordering takeaways or eating out whenever possible. Even if the food is marked as food that is suitable for a Ketogenic Diet, you can never really be sure how someone else has prepared their food or where the ingredients come from. Luckily, there are certainly great Ketogenic choices that can be made when you decide to eat out, but it is still a much better idea to make this a rare occasion rather than something that you have decided to do on a regular basis. Although the beginning may be difficult, the more you focus on making the most of the starting stages of your ketosis journey, the better the results will be in the end.

DAY-1 BREAKFAST

Delicious Mexican Frittata

Serves: 6 / Preparation time: 10 minutes / Cooking time: 20 minutes

8 eggs, scrambled

½ cup cheddar cheese, grated

3 scallions, chopped

1/3 lb tomatoes, sliced

1 small green pepper, chopped

½ cup salsa

2 tsp taco seasoning

½ lb ground beef

1 tbsp olive oil

¼ tsp salt

- Preheat the oven to 190 C/ 375 F.
- Heat olive oil in a medium pan over medium heat. Add ground beef and sauté until brown. Add salsa and taco seasoning and stir well to coat.
- Remove meat from the pan and place on a plate.
- Add green pepper to the pan and cook for few minutes, until crisp.
- Return meat to the pan along with scallions and tomato.
- Add scrambled eggs on top then sprinkle with grated cheese.
- Bake in preheated oven for 20-25 minutes.
- Serve warm and enjoy.

Per Serving: Net Carbs: 3.3g; Calories: 229 Total Fat: 13.8g; Saturated Fat: 5.1g
Protein: 22g; Carbs: 4.4g; Fiber: 1.1g; Sugar: 2.4g; Fat 55% / Protein 39% / Carbs 6%

DAY-1 LUNCH

Tasty Chicken Guacamole Salad

Serves: 03 / Preparation time: 15 minutes / Cooking time: 10 minutes

2 chicken breasts, cooked and cubed

2 serrano chili peppers, chopped

½ cup celery, chopped

½ cup onion, chopped

1 cup cilantro, chopped

1 tbsp fresh lime juice

2 avocados, peeled and pitted

1 tsp kosher salt

Lettuce leaves for serving

- In a bowl, mash avocados with lime juice using a fork.
- Add Serrano chili peppers, onion, cilantro, and salt and stir well to combine.
- Add chicken and fold well.
- Serve salad with lettuce leaves and enjoy.

Per Serving: Net Carbs: 2.4g; Calories: 240; Total Fat: 10.6g; Saturated Fat: 2.7g
Protein: 29.3g; Carbs: 5.2g; Fiber: 2.8g; Sugar: 1.1g; Fat 42% / Protein 51% / Carbs 7%

DAY-1 DINNER

Flavorful Chicken Piccata

Serves: 4 / Preparation time: 15 minutes / Cooking time: 15 minutes

8 chicken thighs, skinless and boneless

2 tbsp fresh parsley, chopped

1 tbsp butter

1 ½ tbsp fresh lemon juice

¾ cup chicken stock

1 thyme sprig

3 garlic cloves, crushed

2 tbsp capers, drained

½ cup dry white wine

3 tbsp olive oil

¼ tsp black pepper

½ tsp kosher salt

- Season chicken with pepper and salt.
- Heat 1 tablespoon of oil in a pan over medium-high heat.
- Add chicken to the pan and cook for 5 minutes.
- Turn chicken to another side. Add thyme, garlic, capers, and wine and cook for 2 minutes.
- Add stock and remaining oil to the pan. Bring to boil. Turn heat to medium and cook for 8 minutes.
- Remove pan from heat. Add butter and lemon juice. Stir well.
- Garnish with parsley and serve.

Per Serving: Net Carbs: 1.9g; Calories: 703; Total Fat: 35.3g; Saturated Fat: 9.4g
Protein: 85g; Carbs: 2.2g; Fiber: 0.3g; Sugar: 0.5g; Fat 47% / Protein 51% / Carbs 2%

DAY-2 BREAKFAST

Healthy Egg Breakfast Muffins

Serves: 6 / Preparation time: 15 minutes / Cooking time: 25 minutes

12 eggs

½ cup fresh spinach, shredded

1 cup cheddar cheese, shredded

¼ cup mushrooms, chopped and sautéed

¼ cup bell pepper, diced

¼ tsp garlic powder

1 cup ham, diced and cooked

2 tbsp onion, chopped

¼ tsp black pepper

½ tsp salt

- Preheat the oven to 176 C/ 350 F.

- Spray 12 cup muffin pan with cooking spray and set aside.

- In a large bowl, beat eggs until well combined.

- Add remaining ingredients to the bowl and mix well together.

- Pour muffin mixture into the prepared muffin tray and bake in preheated oven for 20-25 minutes or until muffin is completely cooked from center.

- Serve and enjoy.

Per Serving: Net Carbs: 2.2g; Calories: 243 Total Fat: 17g; Saturated Fat: 7.4g
Protein: 19.8g; Carbs: 2.8g; Fiber: 0.6g; Sugar: 1.3g; Fat 63% / Protein 33% / Carbs 4%

DAY-2 LUNCH

Creamy Cheesy Cauliflower Mash

Serves: 2 / Preparation time: 10 minutes / Cooking time: 15 minutes

1 cauliflower head, wash and trim

2 oz cheddar cheese, shredded

1 tbsp butter

2 tbsp heavy cream

¼ tsp black pepper

Salt

- Cut cauliflower into the medium size pieces.
- Add cauliflower, butter, and heavy cream in a microwave-safe dish and microwave on high for 6 minutes.
- Stir cauliflower until well coated with cream and butter mixture and microwave for another 6 minutes.
- Transfer cauliflower mixture into the food processor along with shredded cheddar cheese and process until smooth.
- Season with pepper and salt.
- Serve and enjoy.

Per Serving: Net Carbs: 4.5g; Calories: 250; Total Fat: 20.8g; Saturated Fat: 13.1g
Protein: 10.1g; Carbs: 7.8g; Fiber: 3.3g; Sugar: 3.4g; Fat 76% / Protein 17% / Carbs 7%

DAY-2 DINNER

Cauliflower Cheese Casserole

Serves: 6 / Preparation time: 10 minutes / Cooking time: 15 minutes

1 large cauliflower head, cut into florets

1 tsp garlic powder

2 cups cheddar cheese, shredded

2 tsp Dijon mustard

2 oz cream cheese

1 cup heavy cream

½ tsp salt

- Preheat the oven to 190 C/ 375 F.

- Spray 9*9 baking dish with cooking spray and set aside.

- Bring large saucepan of water to boil. Add cauliflower florets and salt and cook until tender.

- Drain cauliflower florets well and place in large bowl. Set aside.

- In a small saucepan, add heavy cream and bring to simmer, stir well.

- Add Dijon mustard and cream cheese and whisk until thickens.

- Remove saucepan from heat. Add 1 cup shredded cheddar cheese and seasonings. Stir well.

- Pour saucepan mixture over cauliflower and stir gently to combine.

- Pour cauliflower mixture into the prepared baking dish and sprinkle with remaining cheese.

- Bake in preheated oven for 15 minutes.

- Serve warm and enjoy.

Per Serving: Net Carbs: 5.5g; Calories: 291; Total Fat: 23.4g; Saturated Fat: 14.7g
Protein: 13.4g; Carbs: 9.1g; Fiber: 3.6g; Sugar: 3.7g; Fat 73% / Protein 19% / Carbs 8%

DAY-3 BREAKFAST

Jalapeno Muffins

Serves: 12 / Preparation time: 10 minutes / Cooking time: 20 minutes

9 eggs

1 jalapeno pepper, sliced

9 oz cheddar cheese, shredded

8 bacon slices, cooked and chopped

¾ cup heavy cream

Pepper

Salt

- Preheat the oven to 176 C/ 350 F.
- Spray 12 cups muffin tray with cooking spray and add cooked bacon slices to each muffin cup.
- In a large bowl, whisk together eggs, shredded cheese, cream, pepper, and salt.
- Pour egg mixture into the prepared muffin cups evenly.
- Now add sliced jalapeno into each muffin cup.
- Bake in preheated oven for 15-20 minutes.
- Serve and enjoy.

Per Serving: Net Carbs: 1g; Calories: 236 Total Fat: 19.1g; Saturated Fat: 9.2g
Protein: 14.9g; Carbs: 1g; Fiber: 0g; Sugar: 0.4g; Fat 73% / Protein 25% / Carbs 2%

DAY-3 LUNCH

Bacon Avocado Chicken Salad

Serves: 4 / Preparation time: 10 minutes / Cooking time: 10 minutes

2 chicken breasts, cooked and chopped

3 tbsp olive oil

3 tbsp fresh lemon juice

1 tsp dried dill

1 tbsp dried chives

4 bacon slices, cooked and chopped

1 cup celery, diced

2 avocado, chopped

½ tsp black pepper

1 tsp salt

- Add all ingredients large mixing bowl and toss well to combine.
- Serve and enjoy.

Per Serving: Net Carbs: 2.9g; Calories: 545; Total Fat: 43.6g; Saturated Fat: 9.8g
Protein: 30.4g; Carbs: 10.2g; Fiber: 7.3g; Sugar: 1.1g; Fat 73% / Protein 23% / Carbs 4%

DAY-3 DINNER

Perfect Bacon Chicken

Serves: 6 / Preparation time: 10 minutes / Cooking time: 40 minutes

6 chicken breasts, cut in half

4 oz cheddar cheese, shredded

½ lb bacon, cut into strips

2 tbsp smoked paprika rub

- Preheat the oven to 204 C/ 400 F.
- Spray large baking tray with cooking spray and set aside.
- Rub chicken breasts from both the sides with smoked paprika rub and place in prepared baking tray.
- Top each chicken breast with bacon slice and bake in preheated oven for 30 minutes.
- After 30 minutes remove baking tray from oven and sprinkle shredded cheese on top of chicken and bacon.
- Return chicken in oven and bake for 10 minutes more or until cheese is bubbly.
- Serve and enjoy.

Per Serving: Net Carbs: 1.2g; Calories: 565; Total Fat: 33.2g; Saturated Fat: 12.2g
Protein: 61.3g; Carbs: 2.1g; Fiber: 0.9g; Sugar: 0.3g; Fat 53% / Protein 45% / Carbs 2%

DAY-4 BREAKFAST

Easy Breakfast Bowl

Serves: 1 / Preparation time: 5 minutes / Cooking time: 15 minutes

2 eggs

½ cup cheddar cheese, shredded

3 bacon strips, cooked and crumbled

½ avocado, sliced

2 tbsp butter

Pepper

Salt

- Melt butter in a pan over medium heat.
- Add eggs into the pan and cook until scrambled. Season with pepper and salt.
- Transfer scrambled egg into the soup bowl.
- Add shredded cheese on top of scramble eggs.
- Top with bacon and avocado slices.
- Serve and enjoy.

Per Serving: Net Carbs: 1.6g; Calories: 603 Total Fat: 54.5g; Saturated Fat: 30g
Protein: 26.4g; Carbs: 3.2g; Fiber: 1.6g; Sugar: 1g; Fat 81% / Protein 18% / Carbs 1%

DAY-4 LUNCH

Creamy Egg Salad

Serves: 4 / Preparation time: 15 minutes / Cooking time: 10 minutes

8 eggs, boiled

2/3 cup mayonnaise

1 tsp yellow mustard

1 green pepper, chopped

2 green onion, chopped

2 celery stalks, chopped

Pepper

Salt

- Peeled and chopped boiled eggs.
- In a mixing bowl, mix together mustard and mayonnaise.
- Add remaining ingredients and stir well to combine.
- Season salad with pepper and salt.
- Serve and enjoy.

Per Serving: Net Carbs: 5.3g; Calories: 266; Total Fat: 22.1g; Saturated Fat: 4.8g
Protein: 11.9g; Carbs: 6.2g; Fiber: 0.9g; Sugar: 3.4g; Fat 75% / Protein 18% / Carbs 7%

DAY-4 DINNER

Quick Cherry Tomato Frittata

Serves: 2 / Preparation time: 10 minutes / Cooking time: ## minutes

6 eggs

1 tbsp chives, chopped

1 tbsp basil, chopped

1 tbsp butter

2/3 cup cherry tomatoes, halved

2/3 cup feta cheese, crumbled

½ onion, sliced

Pepper

Salt

- Preheat the oven to 204 C/ 400 F.
- Melt butter in a pan over medium heat.
- Add sliced onion to the pan and sauté until lightly browned.
- In a bowl, whisk eggs with chives, basil, pepper, and salt.
- Once onion is lightly browned then add egg mixture and cook for 2-3 minutes.
- Top with crumbled feta cheese and cherry tomatoes. Place in preheated oven and cook for 5-7 minutes.
- Serve and enjoy.

Per Serving: Net Carbs: 6.7g; Calories: 394; Total Fat: 29.7g; Saturated Fat: 15.2g
Protein: 24.7g; Carbs: 8.1g; Fiber: 1.4g; Sugar: 5.9g; Fat 68% / Protein 25% / Carbs 7%

DAY-5 BREAKFAST

Egg Breakfast Casserole

Serves: 8 / Preparation time: 10 minutes / Cooking time: 35 minutes

10 eggs

¼ cup goat cheese, crumbled

4 cherry tomatoes, halved

1/3 cup cheddar cheese, grated

1/3 cup ham

1 small zucchini, sliced

½ cup spinach

2/3 cup heavy cream

Pepper

Salt

- Preheat the oven to 176 C/ 350 F.

- Spray 9*13 baking pan with cooking spray and set aside.

- Whisk eggs in a bowl with cream, pepper, and salt.

- Add cheddar cheese, ham, zucchini, and spinach and stir well.

- Pour egg mixture into the prepared pan and top with cherry tomatoes and goat cheese.

- Bake in preheated oven for 30-35 minutes.

- Remove from oven and set aside to cool completely.

- Serve and enjoy.

Per Serving: Net Carbs: 3.7g; Calories: 169 Total Fat: 12.3g; Saturated Fat: 5.6g
Protein: 10.5g; Carbs: 4.6g; Fiber: 0.9g; Sugar: 1.9g; Fat 66% / Protein 25% / Carbs 9%

DAY-5 LUNCH

Chicken Basil Salad

Serves: 1 / Preparation time: 10 minutes / Cooking time: 5 minutes

1 cup chicken breast, cooked and shredded

1 tsp vinegar

1 tbsp sour cream

2 tsp fresh basil, chopped

¼ cup cucumber, diced

Pepper

Salt

- Add all ingredients into the mixing bowl and toss well to combine.
- Season salad with pepper and salt.
- Place in refrigerator for 10 minutes.
- Serve chilled and enjoy.

Per Serving: Net Carbs: 1.4g; Calories: 243; Total Fat: 6.8g; Saturated Fat: 2.8g
Protein: 41.2g; Carbs: 1.6g; Fiber: 0.2g; Sugar: 0.5g; Fat 27% / Protein 69% / Carbs 4%

DAY-5DINNER

Smoked Paprika Chicken

Serves: 4 / Preparation time: 10 minutes / Cooking time: ## minutes

4 chicken breasts, skinless and boneless, cut into chunks

2 tsp garlic, minced

2 tbsp lemon juice

2 tbsp smoked paprika

3 tbsp olive oil

Pepper

Salt

- Preheat the oven to 176 C/ 350 F.
- In a small bowl, mix together garlic, lemon juice, paprika, and olive oil.
- Season chicken with pepper and salt.
- Spread 1/3 bowl mixture on the bottom of casserole dish.
- Add seasoned chicken into the casserole dish and rub with dish sauce.
- Pour remaining sauce on top of chicken and rub well.
- Bake in preheated oven for 30-35 minutes.
- Serve and enjoy.

Per Serving: Net Carbs: 1.2g; Calories: 381; Total Fat: 21.8g; Saturated Fat: 4.6g
Protein: 42.9g; Carbs: 2.6g; Fiber: 1.4g; Sugar: 0.5g; Fat 53% / Protein 45% / Carbs 2%

DAY-6 BREAKFAST

Almond Blueberry Muffins

Serves: 12 / Preparation time: 10 minutes / Cooking time: 20 minutes

3 eggs

¾ cup blueberries

½ tsp vanilla

1/3 cup unsweetened almond milk

1/3 cup coconut oil, melted

1 ½ tsp baking powder, gluten free

½ cup erythritol

2 ½ cups almond flour

¼ tsp sea salt

- Preheat the oven to 176 C/ 350 F.
- Line muffin tray with muffin liners and set aside.
- In a large mixing bowl, mix together almond flour, baking powder, erythritol, and sea salt.
- Add eggs, vanilla, almond milk, and coconut oil and mix well.
- Add blueberries and fold well.
- Pour batter into the prepared muffin tray and bake in preheated oven for 20 minutes.
- Serve and enjoy.

Per Serving: Net Carbs: 2.1g; Calories: 109 Total Fat: 10.2g; Saturated Fat: 5.8g
Protein: 2.7g; Carbs: 3g; Fiber: 0.9g; Sugar: 1.2g; Fat 84% / Protein 9% / Carbs 7%

DAY-6 LUNCH

Mayo Shrimp Cilantro Salad

Serves: 4 / Preparation time: 15 minutes / Cooking time: 10 minutes

1 lb medium shrimp, peeled, deveined, and cooked

2 tbsp fresh lime juice

1 jalapeno pepper, chopped

4 tbsp mayonnaise

2 hard-boiled eggs, chopped

½ green bell pepper, chopped

2 celery stalks, diced

2 radishes, diced

½ onion, diced

Salt

- Add all ingredients into the large mixing bowl and toss well to combine.
- Serve immediately and enjoy.

Per Serving: Net Carbs: 5.9g; Calories: 192; Total Fat: 8.2g; Saturated Fat: 1.4g
Protein: 19.3g; Carbs: 6.2g; Fiber: 0.8g; Sugar: 2.7g; Fat 41% / Protein 43% / Carbs 16%

DAY-6 DINNER

Simple Coconut Shrimp

Serves: 4 / Preparation time: 10 minutes / Cooking time: 10 minutes

1 lb shrimp, deveined

½ cup unsweetened coconut milk

1 tsp garam masala

½ tsp cayenne pepper

½ tsp turmeric

1 tbsp garlic, minced

1 tbsp ginger, minced

1 tsp salt

- Add all ingredients into the saucepan and stir well.
- Heat saucepan over medium heat until shrimp is cooked.
- Stir well and serve with cauliflower rice.

Per Serving: Net Carbs: 4.3g; Calories: 213; Total Fat: 9.2g; Saturated Fat: 7g
Protein: 26.8g; Carbs: 5.3g; Fiber:1 g; Sugar: 1.1g; Fat 40% / Protein 51% / Carbs 9%

DAY-7 BREAKFAST

Cheddar Broccoli Bread

Serves: 10 / Preparation time: 10 minutes / Cooking time: 30 minutes

5 eggs, lightly beaten

2 tsp baking powder, gluten free

3 1/2 tbsp coconut flour

¾ cup broccoli, chopped

1 cup cheddar cheese, shredded

1 tsp salt

- Preheat the oven to 176 C/ 350 F.
- Spray loaf pan with cooking spray and set aside.
- In a mixing bowl, add all ingredients and whisk until well combined.
- Pour egg mixture into the prepared loaf pan.
- Bake in preheated oven for 30-35 minutes.
- Cut into the slices and serve.

Per Serving: Net Carbs: 2g; Calories: 101 Total Fat: 6.7g; Saturated Fat: 3.8g
Protein: 6.5g; Carbs: 4g; Fiber: 2g; Sugar: 0.7g; Fat 62% / Protein 28% / Carbs 10%

DAY-7 LUNCH

Flavorful Tuna Salad

Serves: 8 / Preparation time: 10 minutes / Cooking time: 10 minutes

3 cans tuna, drained and flaked

2 tbsp olive oil

½ lemon juice

¼ cup cilantro, chopped

½ onion, sliced

3 medium avocados, peeled, pitted, and chopped

2 large celery stalks, diced

1/8 tsp pepper

1 tsp sea salt

- Add all ingredients into the large mixing bowl and toss well to combine.
- Serve and enjoy.

Per Serving: Net Carbs: 0.8g; Calories: 183; Total Fat: 10.8g; Saturated Fat: 2g
Protein: 18.3g; Carbs: 2.4g; Fiber: 1.6g; Sugar: 0.6g; Fat 55% / Protein 42% / Carbs 3%

DAY-7 DINNER

Tuna Egg Bake

Serves: 8 / Preparation time: 15 minutes / Cooking time: 45 minutes

6 eggs	1 can tuna, drained
½ tsp dried chilies	2 cups spring greens, chopped
½ tsp garlic powder	1 bell pepper, diced
½ tsp cayenne	2 mushrooms, sliced
½ cup coconut milk	1 medium onion, diced
¼ tsp sea salt	½ tsp pepper
For filling:	¼ tsp sea salt

- Preheat the oven to 176 C/ 350 F.
- In a large bowl, whisk together eggs, coconut milk, dried chilies, sea salt, garlic powder, and cayenne.
- Spray oven safe pan with cooking spray and heat over medium heat.
- Add mushroom and onion to the pan and sauté until soften.
- Add bell peppers and cook for 4 minutes more.
- Add spring green and cook until wilted.
- Add tuna and stir until well combined.
- Now add egg mixture. Place in preheated oven and cook for 40-45 minutes.
- Serve and enjoy.

Per Serving: Net Carbs: 3.1g; Calories: 138; Total Fat: 8.8g; Saturated Fat: 4.6g
Protein: 11.1g; Carbs: 4.4g; Fiber: 1.3g; Sugar: 2.3g; Fat 58% / Protein 33% / Carbs 9%

DAY-8 BREAKFAST

Delicious Ricotta Omelet

Serves: 1 / Preparation time: 10 minutes / Cooking time: 10 minutes

3 eggs

2 tbsp sun-dried tomatoes, chopped

2 tbsp mozzarella cheese, shredded

1 tbsp fresh basil, chopped

2 tbsp ricotta whole milk

1 tsp butter

- Melt butter in a pan over medium heat.
- Meanwhile, in a bowl, whisk together eggs, sun-dried tomatoes, and basil.
- Pour egg mixture into the pan. Cover pan with lid and cook over medium-low heat.
- Mix together mozzarella cheese and ricotta.
- Remove pan lid and add mozzarella mixture on top of omelet.
- Cover pan again and cook for 1-2 minutes or until omelet cooked through.
- Transfer omelet onto a serving plate and fold it and serve.

Per Serving: Net Carbs: 4.6g; Calories: 441 Total Fat: 31g; Saturated Fat: 15.1g
Protein: 36.4g; Carbs: 4.9g; Fiber: 0.3g; Sugar: 1.7g; Fat 63% / Protein 33% / Carbs 4%

DAY-8 LUNCH

Flavorful Citrusy Shrimp

Serves: 3 / Preparation time: 10 minutes / Cooking time: 10 minutes

1 lb shrimp

1 tbsp fresh parsley, chopped

1 tsp lemon zest

1 tbsp fresh lemon juice

3 garlic cloves, minced

2 tbsp olive oil

½ tsp black pepper

½ tsp sea salt

- Season shrimp with pepper and salt.
- Heat olive oil in a pan over medium heat.
- Add garlic to the pan and sauté until brown.
- Add shrimp and sauté for 1 minute.
- Add lemon zest and lemon juice and stir well. Cook shrimp over medium heat until cooked through.
- Garnish with parsley and serve.

Per Serving: Net Carbs: 3.6g; Calories: 267; Total Fat: 12g; Saturated Fat: 2.2g
Protein: 34.8g; Carbs: 3.9g; Fiber: 0.3g; Sugar: 0.2g; Fat 41% / Protein 53% / Carbs 6%

DAY-8 DINNER

Simple Old Bay Seasoned Shrimp

Serves: 1 / Preparation time: 5 minutes / Cooking time: 10 minutes

---

32 oz shrimp, peeled and deveined   1 tbsp olive oil

½ lemon juice

2 tbsp old bay seasoning

- Add all ingredients into the large bowl and toss until well coated.
- Heat large pan over medium-high heat.
- Add shrimp into the pan and cook for 2 minutes on each side.
- Serve with zoodles and enjoy.

Per Serving: Net Carbs: 3.6g; Calories: 301; Total Fat: 7.4g; Saturated Fat: 1.7g
Protein: 51.7g; Carbs: 3.6g; Fiber: 0g; Sugar: 0.1g; Fat 24% / Protein 70% / Carbs 6%

DAY-9 BREAKFAST

Olive Bacon Quiche

Serves: 8 / Preparation time: 10 minutes / Cooking time: 30 minutes

12 eggs, whisked

¾ cup coconut cream

3 garlic cloves, minced

¼ cup fresh basil leaves

15 olives, diced

2 small tomatoes, diced

4 cups spinach, chopped

1 onion, diced

2 bell peppers, diced

6 bacon slices, diced

3 tbsp coconut oil

Pepper

Salt

- Preheat the oven 176 C/ 350 F.
- Melt coconut oil in a large pan over medium-high heat.
- Add bacon and cook for 3-4 minutes or until crispy. Remove from pan and set aside.
- Add onion and bell pepper in same pan and sauté for 5 minutes.
- Add spinach and sauté for 1-2 minutes.
- Remove pan from heat and set aside.
- In a large mixing bowl, mix together eggs, bacon, coconut cream, garlic, basil, olives, tomato, and spinach mixture. Season with pepper and salt.
- Pour egg mixture into the 9" baking dish and bake in preheated oven for 30 minutes.
- Serve and enjoy.

Per Serving: Net Carbs: 5.7g; Calories: 301 Total Fat: 24.1g; Saturated Fat: 13.3g
Protein: 15.3g; Carbs: 7.8g; Fiber: 2.1g; Sugar: 4g; Fat 72% / Protein 20% / Carbs 8%

DAY-9 LUNCH

Easy Cabbage Noodles

Serves: 4 / Preparation time: 10 minutes / Cooking time: 10 minutes

1 lb cabbage, cored and cut into strips

2 tbsp butter

2 garlic cloves, sliced

¼ cup onion, sliced

Pepper

Salt

- Melt butter in a pan over medium heat.

- Add garlic, onion, and cabbage and sauté for 10 minutes or until cabbage is tender.

- Season with pepper and salt.

- Serve and enjoy.

Per Serving: Net Carbs: 4.8g; Calories: 84; Total Fat: 5.9g; Saturated Fat: 3.7g
Protein: 1.7g; Carbs: 7.8g; Fiber: 3g; Sugar: 4g; Fat 65% / Protein 10% / Carbs 25%

DAY-9 DINNER

Cauliflower Cheese Casserole

Serves: 8 / Preparation time: 15 minutes / Cooking time: 30 minutes

6 tbsp fresh chives, chopped

1 cup cheddar cheese, shredded

1 cup Monterey jack cheese, shredded

1 tbsp ranch seasoning

½ cup mayonnaise

½ cup sour cream

1 large head cauliflower, cut into florets

8 bacon slices, cooked and crumbled

¼ tsp pepper

- Preheat the oven to 187 C/ 370 F.
- Spray 13*9 baking dish with cooking spray and set aside.
- Steam cauliflower florets for 15-20 minutes or until tender.
- In a large bowl, combine together sour cream, ranch seasoning, mayonnaise, and black pepper.
- Add steam cauliflower, 3 tbsp chives, 1 cup cheddar cheese, and half of bacon into the bowl and mix well.
- Pour mixture into the prepared baking dish and top with Monterey jack cheese and remaining bacon.
- Cover dish with foil and bake in preheated oven for 20 minutes.
- Remove foil and bake for 10 minutes more.
- Garnish with remaining chives and serve.

Per Serving: Net Carbs: 4.2g; Calories: 364; Total Fat: 30g; Saturated Fat: 11.7g
Protein: 16.6g; Carbs: 6.9g; Fiber: 2.7g; Sugar: 2.7g; Fat 75% / Protein 19% / Carbs 6%

DAY-10 BREAKFAST

Coconut Waffles

Serves: 4 / Preparation time: 10 minutes / Cooking time: 10 minutes

4 eggs

1 ½ tsp baking powder

4 tbsp coconut flour

1 tbsp powdered stevia

1 tsp vanilla

1 tbsp butter, melted

4 oz cream cheese

- Preheat the waffle iron.
- Add all ingredients into the blender and blend until smooth.
- Spray waffle iron with cooking spray.
- Pour ¼ cup batter for each waffle in hot waffle maker and cook according to the waffle iron instructions.
- Serve and enjoy.

Per Serving: Net Carbs: 3.6g; Calories: 227 Total Fat: 18.4g; Saturated Fat: 10.4g
Protein: 9.2g; Carbs: 6.6g; Fiber: 3g; Sugar: 1g; Fat 74% / Protein 18% / Carbs 8%

DAY-10 LUNCH

Curried Chicken Salad

Serves: 4 / Preparation time: 10 minutes / Cooking time: 10 minutes

2 oz walnuts, chopped

2 tbsp green onion, chopped

8 oz chicken, cooked and diced

For dressing:

2 tbsp fresh cilantro, chopped

1/8 tsp cayenne

1 tsp curry powder

1 tbsp lemon juice

½ cup mayonnaise

¼ tsp pepper

¼ tsp salt

- In a small bowl, mix together all dressing ingredients and set aside.
- Add walnuts, green onion, and chicken into the large mixing bowl and mix well.
- Pour dressing over salad and toss well to coat.
- Serve and enjoy.

Per Serving: Net Carbs: 0.9g; Calories: 372; Total Fat: 31.5g; Saturated Fat: 4.7g
Protein: 18.6g; Carbs: 2.4g; Fiber: 1.5g; Sugar: 0.5g; Fat 78% / Protein 20% / Carbs 2%

DAY-10 DINNER

Cheese Broccoli Soup

Serves: 8 / Preparation time: 10 minutes / Cooking time: 15 minutes

4 cups broccoli, cut into florets

3 1/2 cups vegetable broth

2 garlic cloves, minced

1 tbsp olive oil

3 cups cheddar cheese, shredded

1 cup heavy cream

Pepper

Salt

- Heat olive oil in a large pot over medium heat.

- Add garlic and sauté for a minute.

- Add broth, broccoli, and heavy cream and bring to boil, reduce heat and simmer for 15 minutes.

- Add shredded cheese and stir continuously until cheese is melted.

- Season with pepper and salt.

- Remove from heat and serve.

Per Serving: Net Carbs: 3.4g; Calories: 271; Total Fat: 22.1g; Saturated Fat: 12.8g
Protein: 14.3g; Carbs: 4.6g; Fiber: 1.2g; Sugar: 1.3g; Fat 73% / Protein 22% / Carbs 5%

DAY-11 BREAKFAST

Easy Egg Loaf

Serves: 4 / Preparation time: 5 minutes / Cooking time: 30 minutes

4 eggs

1 tsp swerve

1 tsp vanilla

4 oz cream cheese

4 tbsp butter

- Add all ingredients into the small bowl and mix with electric mixer until well combined and smooth.
- Spray 9*13 baking pan with cooking spray.
- Pour batter into the prepared pan and bake at 176 C/ 350 F for 30 minutes.
- Serve and enjoy.

Per Serving: Net Carbs: 1.7g; Calories: 268 Total Fat: 25.8g; Saturated Fat: 14.9g
Protein: 7.8g; Carbs: 1.7g; Fiber: 0g; Sugar: 0.5g; Fat 86% / Protein 12% / Carbs 2%

DAY-11 LUNCH

Almond Chicken Salad

Serves: 2 / Preparation time: 15 minutes / Cooking time: 5 minutes

2 cups chicken breasts, cooked and diced

1 tsp curry powder

2 medium celery stalks, chopped

2 tbsp almonds, chopped

¼ cup mayonnaise

Salt

- Add all ingredients into the large bowl and toss well to combine.
- Serve and enjoy.

Per Serving: Net Carbs: 1.3g; Calories: 490; Total Fat: 33.6g; Saturated Fat: 6.1g
Protein: 42.2g; Carbs: 3g; Fiber: 1.7g; Sugar: 0.8g; Fat 63% / Protein 35% / Carbs 2%

DAY-11 DINNER

Shrimp Mushroom Soup

Serves: 8 / Preparation time: 10 minutes / Cooking time: 15 minutes

24 oz shrimp, cooked	½ cup butter
32 oz chicken broth	1 cup heavy whipping cream
2 cups mushrooms, sliced	Pepper
8 oz cheddar cheese, shredded	Salt

- Add broth and mushrooms to a large pot. Bring to boil over high heat.
- Turn heat to medium and add cheese, whipping cream, and butter and stir until cheese is melted.
- Reduce heat and add shrimp. Stir well and cook for 2 minutes more.
- Serve and enjoy.

Per Serving: Net Carbs: 2.9g; Calories: 391; Total Fat: 28.6g; Saturated Fat: 17.3g
Protein: 29.7g; Carbs: 3.1g; Fiber: 0.2g; Sugar: 0.8g; Fat 66% / Protein 31% / Carbs 3%

DAY-12 BREAKFAST

Delicious Breakfast Cookies

Serves: 8 / Preparation time: 10 minutes / Cooking time: 25 minutes

3 eggs

1 cup cheddar cheese, shredded

6 bacon slices, cooked and crumbled

¼ lb sausage, cooked and crumbled

½ tsp garlic powder

2 tsp baking powder

6 tbsp coconut flour

8 oz cream cheese, softened

½ tsp black pepper

¾ tsp salt

- Preheat the oven to 176 C/ 350 F.
- Spray baking tray with cooking spray and line with parchment paper. Set aside.
- In a large bowl, beat together eggs and cream cheese until smooth.
- Add coconut flour, garlic powder, baking powder, pepper and salt and beat until well combined.
- Add cheese, bacon, and sausage and stir well.
- Spoon cookie mixture into eight mounds onto a prepared baking tray and using hands press down to 1 inch thickness.
- Bake in preheated oven for 20-25 minutes or until lightly golden brown.
- Remove from oven and set aside to cool completely.
- Serve and enjoy.

Per Serving: Net Carbs: 3.1g; Calories: 329 Total Fat: 26.9g; Saturated Fat: 13.7g
Protein: 16.6g; Carbs: 5.1g; Fiber: 2g; Sugar: 0.7g; Fat 72% / Protein 25% / Carbs 3%

DAY-12 LUNCH

Cucumber Tuna Salad

Serves: 2 / Preparation time: 10 minutes / Cooking time: 5 minutes

2 cans tuna water packed

½ lime juice

1/3 cup mayonnaise

½ cucumber, peeled and chopped

¼ small onion, chopped

1 celery stalk, chopped

Pepper

Salt

- Add all ingredients into the mixing bowl and mix until well combined.
- Serve and enjoy.

Per Serving: Net Carbs: 4.4g; Calories: 592; Total Fat: 41.2g; Saturated Fat: 7g
Protein: 48g; Carbs: 5.6g; Fiber: 1.2g; Sugar: 2g; Fat 63% / Protein 34% / Carbs 3%

DAY-12 DINNER

Delicious Ranch Chicken

Serves: 6 / Preparation time: 10 minutes / Cooking time: 6 hours

2 lbs chicken, skinless and boneless

3 tbsp butter

4 oz cream cheese

3 tbsp dry ranch dressing

Pepper

Salt

- Season chicken with pepper and salt and place into the slow cooker.
- Add butter and cheese over the chicken.
- Sprinkle dry ranch dressing over the chicken.
- Cover slow cooker with lid and cook on low for 6 hours.
- Shred the chicken using fork and serve.

Per Serving: Net Carbs: 0.9g; Calories: 347; Total Fat: 17g; Saturated Fat: 9.1g
Protein: 45.4g; Carbs: 0.9g; Fiber: 0g; Sugar: 0.2g; Fat 46% / Protein 52% / Carbs 2%

DAY-13 BREAKFAST

Bacon Cheese Bread

Serves: 10 / Preparation time: 10 minutes / Cooking time: 50 minutes

---

½ lb bacon, diced

1 cup cheddar cheese, grated

2 eggs

1/3 cup sour cream

4 tbsp butter, melted

1 tbsp baking powder

1 1/2 cups almond flour

- Preheat the oven to 150 C/ 300 F.

- Spray loaf pan with cooking spray and set aside.

- Cook bacon in a pan over medium heat until crispy.

- Meanwhile, in a large bowl, mix together almond flour and baking powder.

- In another bowl, whisk together eggs and sour cream until smooth.

- Pour egg mixture into the almond flour and mix until combined.

- Add cheese, bacon, and butter and fold well.

- Pour bread mixture into the prepared loaf pan and bake in preheated oven for 45-50 minutes.

- Slices and serve.

Per Serving: Net Carbs: 2g; Calories: 263 Total Fat: 22.4g; Saturated Fat: 9.8g
Protein: 13.5g; Carbs: 2.5g; Fiber: 0.5g; Sugar: 0.3g; Fat 76% / Protein 20% / Carbs 4%

DAY-13 LUNCH

Chili Garlic Shrimp

Serves: 2 / Preparation time: 10 minutes / Cooking time: 10 minutes

1 lb shrimp, cooked

1 tsp cumin powder

1 tsp chili powder

2 garlic cloves, minced

½ bell pepper, chopped

3 tbsp olive oil

- Heat a large pan over medium heat.
- Add all ingredients into the pan and sauté until bell pepper are cooked.
- Serve and enjoy.

Per Serving: Net Carbs: 5.9g; Calories: 468 Total Fat: 25.4g; Saturated Fat: 4.2g
Protein: 52.5g; Carbs: 7g; Fiber: 1.1g; Sugar: 0.8g; Fat 50% / Protein 45% / Carbs 5%

DAY-13 DINNER

Pesto Cheese Salmon

Serves: 2 / Preparation time: 10 minutes / Cooking time: 20 minutes

2 salmon fillets

¼ cup parmesan cheese, grated

For pesto:

2 garlic cloves, peeled and chopped

¼ cup olive oil

1 ½ cups fresh basil leaves

¼ cup parmesan cheese, grated

¼ cup pine nuts

½ tsp black pepper

½ tsp salt

- Add all pesto ingredients to the blender and blend until smooth.
- Preheat the oven to 204 C/ 400 F.
- Place salmon fillet on a baking tray and spread 2 tablespoons of the pesto on each salmon fillet.
- Sprinkle grated cheese on top of pesto.
- Bake in preheated oven for 20 minutes.
- Serve and enjoy.

Per Serving: Net Carbs: 2.9g; Calories: 726; Total Fat: 57g; Saturated Fat: 12g
Protein: 49.7g; Carbs: 4g; Fiber: 1.1g; Sugar: 0.7g; Fat 71% / Protein 28% / Carbs 1%

DAY-14 BREAKFAST

Coconut Chia Pudding

Serves: 1 / Preparation time: 5 minutes / Cooking time: 5 minutes

2 tbsp chia seeds

¾ cup coconut milk

½ tsp vanilla

1 fresh strawberry, sliced

- Add all ingredients except strawberry into the glass jar and mix well.
- Cover jar with lid and place in refrigerator for overnight.
- Top with sliced strawberry and serve.

Per Serving: Net Carbs: 6.1g; Calories: 173 Total Fat: 13.6g; Saturated Fat: 8g
Protein: 4.3g; Carbs: 6.3g; Fiber: 0.2g; Sugar: 0.9g; Fat 73% / Protein 12% / Carbs 15%

DAY-14 LUNCH

Avocado Bacon Soup

Serves: 4 / Preparation time: 10 minutes / Cooking time: 10 minutes

½ lb bacon, cooked and chopped

½ lime juice

2 avocados, pitted

1 tsp garlic powder

1/3 cup fresh cilantro, chopped

4 cups chicken stock

Pepper

Salt

- Add chicken stock into the saucepan and bring to boil over low heat.
- Add avocados, lime juice, garlic powder, and cilantro into the blender.
- Add 1 cup warm chicken stock into the blender and blend until smooth.
- Remove saucepan from heat.
- Add blended avocado mixture and bacon into the saucepan and stir well.
- Season soup with pepper and salt.
- Serve warm and enjoy.

Per Serving: Net Carbs: 2.4g; Calories: 351; Total Fat: 26.8g; Saturated Fat: 8.4g
Protein: 22.4g; Carbs: 4.1g; Fiber: 1.7g; Sugar: 1g; Fat 70% / Protein 27% / Carbs 3%

DAY-14 DINNER

Lemon Parmesan Salmon

Serves: 4 / Preparation time: 10 minutes / Cooking time: 15 minutes

4 salmon fillets

¼ cup parmesan cheese, grated

½ cup walnuts

1 tsp olive oil

1 tbsp lemon rind

- Preheat the oven to 204 C/ 400 F.
- Spray a baking tray with cooking spray.
- Place salmon on a baking tray.
- Add walnuts into the food processor and process until finely ground.
- Mix ground walnuts with parmesan cheese, oil, and lemon rind. Stir well.
- Spread walnut mixture over the salmon fillets and press gently.
- Bake in preheated oven for 15 minutes.
- Serve and enjoy.

Per Serving: Net Carbs: 0.7g; Calories: 493; Total Fat: 30.4g; Saturated Fat: 8.3g
Protein: 50.4g; Carbs: 1.9g; Fiber: 1.2g; Sugar: 0.3g; Fat 57% / Protein 42% / Carbs 1%

DAY-15 BREAKFAST

Spinach Bacon Frittata

Serves: 4 / Preparation time: 10 minutes / Cooking time: 30 minutes

8 eggs

5 oz cheddar cheese, shredded

1 cup heavy whipping cream

8 oz fresh spinach

2 tbsp butter

5 oz bacon, diced

Pepper

Salt

- Preheat the oven to 176 C/ 350 F.

- Spray 9*9 baking dish with cooking spray and set aside.

- Melt butter in a pan over medium heat.

- Add bacon in a pan and cook until crispy.

- Add spinach and cook until wilted. Remove pan from heat and set aside.

- In a bowl, whisk together heavy whipping cream and eggs.

- Pour cream and egg mixture into the prepared dish.

- Add bacon and spinach into the egg mixture and top with shredded cheddar cheese.

- Bake in preheated oven for 25-30 minutes.

- Serve and enjoy.

Per Serving: Net Carbs: 3.3g; Calories: 628 Total Fat: 52.4g; Saturated Fat: 25.7g
Protein: 35.3g; Carbs: 4.6g; Fiber: 1.3g; Sugar: 1.1g; Fat 75% / Protein 23% / Carbs 2%

DAY-15 LUNCH

Italian Pepperoni Avocado Salad

Serves: 1 / Preparation time: 5 minutes / Cooking time: 5 minutes

1 oz mozzarella pearls

15 pepperoni slices

½ avocado, cubed

½ tbsp fresh lime juice

1 tsp Italian seasoning

Pepper

Salt

- Add all ingredients into the small bowl and toss well to combine.
- Serve and enjoy.

Per Serving: Net Carbs: 0.7g; Calories: 524; Total Fat: 45.2g; Saturated Fat: 16.5g
Protein: 24.3g; Carbs: 2.2g; Fiber: 1.5g; Sugar: 0.4g; Fat 79% / Protein 20% / Carbs 1%

DAY-15 DINNER

Garlic Onion Pork Tenderloin

Serves: 6 / Preparation time: 10 minutes / Cooking time: 30 minutes

2 lbs pork tenderloin

For rub:

1 tbsp onion powder

1 tbsp smoked paprika

1 tbsp garlic powder

½ tbsp salt

- Preheat the oven to 218 C/ 425 F.

- In a small bowl, combine together all rub ingredients and rub over pork tenderloin.

- Heat oven-safe pan over medium-high heat.

- Spray pan with cooking spray. Sear pork on all sides until lightly golden brown.

- Place pan into the preheated oven and roast for about 25-30 minutes.

- Cut into slices and serve.

Per Serving: Net Carbs: 2g; Calories: 228; Total Fat: 5.5g; Saturated Fat: 1.8g
Protein: 40.1g; Carbs: 2.6g; Fiber: 0.6g; Sugar: 0.9g; Fat 24% / Protein 71% / Carbs 5%

DAY-16 BREAKFAST

Healthy Coconut Porridge

Serves: 1 / Preparation time: 5 minutes / Cooking time: 10 minutes

1 egg

4 tbsp coconut cream

1 tbsp coconut flour

1 oz coconut oil

Pinch of salt

- Add all ingredients into the small saucepan and stir well.
- Cook over low heat until get desired consistency.
- Top with fresh berries or coconut flakes.
- Serve and enjoy.

Per Serving: Net Carbs: 4.4g; Calories: 475 Total Fat: 47.8g; Saturated Fat: 39.1g
Protein: 7.9g; Carbs: 8.7g; Fiber: 4.3g; Sugar: 2.3g; Fat 90% / Protein 7% / Carbs 3%

DAY-16 LUNCH

Cilantro Shrimp Avocado Salad

Serves: 6 / Preparation time: 10 minutes / Cooking time: 10 minutes

1 lb shrimp, cooked

2 cups lettuce, chopped

2 avocados, chopped

2 cups spinach

For dressing:

3 tbsp fresh lime juice

½ cup fresh cilantro, chopped

2 tbsp olive oil

1/8 tsp black pepper

Pinch of salt

- In a small bowl, combine together all dressing ingredients and set aside.

- Add shrimp into the large mixing bowl. Pour dressing over shrimp and toss well.

- Place shrimp in refrigerator for 1 hour.

- Add lettuce, avocados, and spinach into the shrimp and toss well.

- Serve and enjoy.

Per Serving: Net Carbs: 3.1g; Calories: 272; Total Fat: 19.1g; Saturated Fat: 3.8g
Protein: 18.9g; Carbs: 8g; Fiber: 4.9g; Sugar: 0.6g; Fat 65% / Protein 29% / Carbs 6%

DAY-16 DINNER

Lemon Garlic Chicken

Serves: 4 / Preparation time: 10 minutes / Cooking time: 40 minutes

2 lbs chicken drumsticks

1 fresh lemon juice

10 garlic cloves, sliced

2 tbsp olive oil

4 tbsp butter

2 tbsp parsley, chopped

Pepper

Salt

- Preheat the oven to 225 C/ 450 F.
- Grease baking tray with butter then place chicken pieces in butter greased pan.
- Season chicken with pepper and salt.
- Sprinkle the parsley and garlic over the chicken.
- Pour lemon juice and olive oil on top of chicken.
- Bake chicken in preheated oven for 35-40 minutes.
- Serve and enjoy.

Per Serving: Net Carbs: 2.6g; Calories: 560; Total Fat: 31.6g; Saturated Fat: 11.8g
Protein: 63.1g; Carbs: 2.9g; Fiber: 0.3g; Sugar: 0.4g; Fat 52% / Protein 46% / Carbs 2%

DAY-17 BREAKFAST

Bacon Avocado Quiche

Serves: 6 / Preparation time: 10 minutes / Cooking time: 30 minutes

6 eggs

1 avocado, peeled and chopped

½ cup bacon, cooked and crumbled

½ cup mozzarella cheese

¼ cup coconut milk

¼ tsp black pepper

¼ tsp salt

- Preheat the oven to 176 C/ 350 F.
- Spray pie dish with cooking spray and set aside.
- In a large bowl, whisk together eggs, coconut milk, pepper and salt until well combined.
- Add avocado, bacon and cheese and stir well.
- Pour egg mixture into the prepared pie dish and bake in preheated oven for 30 minutes.
- Serve and enjoy.

Per Serving: Net Carbs: 1.5g; Calories: 255 Total Fat: 20.4g; Saturated Fat: 6.2g
Protein: 14.7g; Carbs: 3.8g; Fiber: 2.3g; Sugar: 0.6g; Fat 73% / Protein 24% / Carbs 3%

DAY-17 LUNCH

Perfect Geek Salad

Serves: 6 / Preparation time: 10 minutes / Cooking time: 5 minutes

2 cucumbers, peeled and chopped

2 tbsp olive oil

2 tbsp fresh dill, chopped

4 oz feta cheese, cubed

2 cups grape tomatoes, halved

Pepper

Salt

- Add all ingredients into the mixing bowl and toss well to combine.
- Serve and enjoy.

Per Serving: Net Carbs: 5.9g; Calories: 118; Total Fat: 9g; Saturated Fat: 3.6g
Protein: 4.1g; Carbs: 7.3g; Fiber: 1.4g; Sugar: 4g; Fat 67% / Protein 13% / Carbs 20%

DAY-17 DINNER

Zucchini Cheese Casserole

Serves: 6 / Preparation time: 10 minutes / Cooking time: 25 minutes

4 cup zucchini, grated

1/2 cup parmesan cheese, grated

2 eggs

1 tbsp garlic, minced

1/2 cup onion, diced

1/2 cup cheddar cheese, shredded

1 cup mozzarella cheese, shredded

1/2 tsp salt

- Preheat the oven to 375 F.

- Spray baking dish with cooking spray and set aside.

- Add zucchini and salt into the colander and set aside for 10 minutes.

- Squeeze out all liquid from zucchini.

- In a large mixing bowl, combine together zucchini, cheddar cheese, mozzarella cheese, 1/2 parmesan cheese, eggs, garlic, and onion and pour into the prepared baking dish.

- Bake in preheated oven for 25 minutes.

- Serve and enjoy.

Per Serving: Net Carbs: 3.2g; Calories: 140; Total Fat: 8.6g; Saturated Fat: 5g
Protein: 10.7g; Carbs: 4.3g; Fiber: 1.1g; Sugar: 1.9g; Fat 58% / Protein 32% / Carbs 10%

DAY-18 BREAKFAST

Healthy Spinach Quiche

Serves: 6 / Preparation time: 15 minutes / Cooking time: 40 minutes

6 eggs

1 tsp lemon zest

Pinch of nutmeg

8 oz cheddar cheese, grated

¾ cup heavy cream

2 oz onion, sliced

16 oz frozen spinach, thawed and squeezed

1/3 lb bacon, cooked and chopped

¼ tsp pepper

¾ tsp salt

- Spray 8*8 pie dish with cooking spray and set aside.
- Preheat the oven to 176 C/ 350 F.
- In a large mixing bowl, add all ingredients and mix using electric mixer until well combined.
- Pour quiche mixture into the prepared pie dish and bake in preheated oven for 40 minutes.
- Serve and enjoy.

Per Serving: Net Carbs: 3.5g; Calories: 425 Total Fat: 33.3g; Saturated Fat: 16.3g
Protein: 26.9g; Carbs: 5.4g; Fiber: 1.9g; Sugar: 1.3g; Fat 70% / Protein 26% / Carbs 4%

DAY-18 LUNCH

Healthy Mediterranean Salad

Serves: 6 / Preparation time: 10 minutes / Cooking time: 10 minutes

½ cup feta cheese, crumbled

1/3 cup onion, sliced

1 cup artichoke hearts, chopped

2 cups cucumber, chopped

2 cups grape tomatoes, halved

For dressing:

1 garlic clove, minced

4 tsp apple cider vinegar

2 tbsp sun-dried tomatoes

6 tbsp olive oil

1/8 tsp black pepper

¼ tsp sea salt

- Add olive oil, garlic, vinegar, sun-dried tomatoes, pepper, and salt into the blender and blend until smooth.

- In a large mixing bowl, mix together feta cheese, onion, artichoke hearts, cucumber, and grape tomatoes.

- Pour dressing over salad and toss well to combine.

- Serve and enjoy.

Per Serving: Net Carbs: 5.3g; Calories: 186; Total Fat: 16.9g; Saturated Fat: 3.9g
Protein: 3.5g; Carbs: 7.7g; Fiber: 2.4g; Sugar: 3.6g; Fat 81% / Protein 7% / Carbs 12%

DAY-18 DINNER

Tasty Pumpkin Spiced Soup

Serves: 4 / Preparation time: 10 minutes / Cooking time: 45 minutes

1 cup pumpkin puree

4 tbsp butter

1 1/2 cups vegetable broth

1/2 cup heavy cream

1 bay leaf

1/8 tsp nutmeg

1/4 tsp coriander

1/2 tsp ginger, minced

2 garlic cloves, minced

1/4 onion, chopped

1/4 tsp cinnamon

1/2 tsp pepper

1/2 tsp salt

- Melt butter in a saucepan over medium-low heat.
- Add ginger, garlic, and onion to the pan and sauté for 2-3 minutes.
- Add spices and stir well and cook for 2 minutes.
- Add broth and pumpkin puree and stir well.
- Bring to boil then reduce heat to low and simmer for 20 minutes.
- Puree the soup using immersion blender until smooth then simmer for another 20 minutes.
- Remove pan from heat and add heavy cream and stir well.
- Serve and enjoy.

Per Serving: Net Carbs: 5.2g; Calories: 196; Total Fat: 17.8g; Saturated Fat: 11g
Protein: 3.2g; Carbs: 7.3g; Fiber: 2.1 g; Sugar: 2.7g; Fat 83% / Protein 7% / Carbs 10%

DAY-19 BREAKFAST

Almond Pumpkin Pancake

Serves: 4 / Preparation time: 10 minutes / Cooking time: 10 minutes

4 eggs

2 tbsp butter

2 tsp liquid stevia

1 tsp baking powder

½ tsp cinnamon

½ cup pumpkin puree

1 cup almond flour

- In a bowl, whisk together almond flour, stevia, baking powder, cinnamon, pumpkin puree, and eggs until well combined.
- Melt ½ tablespoon of butter in a pan over medium heat.
- Pour a heaping spoonful pancake batter into the melted butter and make round pancake.
- Cook pancake until lightly browned from both the sides.
- Serve and enjoy.

Per Serving: Net Carbs: 3.3g; Calories: 166 Total Fat: 13.7g; Saturated Fat: 5.3g
Protein: 7.5g; Carbs: 5.1g; Fiber: 1.8g; Sugar: 1.6g; Fat 74% / Protein 18% / Carbs 8%

DAY-19 LUNCH

Refreshing Creamy Cucumber Salad

Serves: 6 / Preparation time: 10 minutes / Cooking time: 5 minutes

3 cucumbers, peeled and sliced

2 tbsp fresh chives, chopped

2 tbsp mayonnaise

½ cup sour cream

1 small onion, sliced

Pepper

Salt

- Add all ingredients into the large mixing bowl and mix well to combine.
- Place in refrigerator for 30 minutes.
- Serve chilled and enjoy.

Per Serving: Net Carbs: 6.2g; Calories: 69; Total Fat: 4.4g; Saturated Fat: 1.1g
Protein: 1.4g; Carbs: 7.2g; Fiber: 1g; Sugar: 3g; Fat 57% / Protein 8% / Carbs 35%

DAY-19 DINNER

Herb Chicken

Serves: 10 / Preparation time: 10 minutes / Cooking time: 4 hours

6 chicken breasts, skinless and boneless

1/2 tsp thyme

1 tsp dried oregano

4 garlic cloves

1 medium onion, sliced

14 oz can tomatoes, diced

1 tsp dried basil

1 tsp dried rosemary

1 tbsp olive oil

1/2 cup balsamic vinegar

Pepper

Salt

- Add all ingredients into the slow cooker and stir well.
- Cover slow cooker with lid and cook on high for 4 hours.
- Stir well and serve.

Per Serving: Net Carbs: 2.7g; Calories: 197; Total Fat: 8g; Saturated Fat: 2g
Protein: 25.9g; Carbs: 3.8g; Fiber: 1.1g; Sugar: 1.9g; Fat 39% / Protein 55% / Carbs 6%

DAY-20 BREAKFAST

Blueberry Almond Coconut Flour Casserole

Serves: 12 / Preparation time: 10 minutes / Cooking time: 25 minutes

3 eggs

1 cup blueberries

½ tsp vanilla

1 ¼ cup coconut milk

8 drops liquid stevia

½ tsp baking soda

1 ½ tsp baking powder

¼ cup coconut flour

1 1/2 cup almond flour

½ tsp salt

- Preheat the oven to 190 C/ 375 F.

- Spray 9*13 baking dish with cooking spray and set aside.

- In a large bowl, whisk together almond flour, baking soda, baking powder, coconut flour, and salt.

- Make in the center of almond flour mixture. Add eggs, coconut milk, vanilla, and stevia. Mix until well combined.

- Add blueberries and fold well.

- Pour into the prepared baking dish and bake in preheated oven for 20-25 minutes.

- Serve and enjoy.

Per Serving: Net Carbs: 3.5g; Calories: 111 Total Fat: 9.2g; Saturated Fat: 6.1g
Protein: 3.1g; Carbs: 5.6g; Fiber: 2.1g; Sugar: 2.4g; Fat 75% / Protein 12% / Carbs 13%

DAY-20 LUNCH

Delicious Zucchini Soup

Serves: 4 / Preparation time: 10 minutes / Cooking time: 20 minutes

3 medium zucchini, chopped

2 tbsp sour cream

32 oz chicken broth

2 garlic cloves

½ small onion, quartered

Pepper

Salt

- Add broth, zucchini, garlic, and onion to the saucepan and heat over medium heat. Bring to boil.

- Turn heat to low and simmer for 20 minutes.

- Puree the soup using immersion blender until smooth and creamy.

- Add sour cream and stir well.

- Season soup with pepper and salt.

- Serve hot and enjoy.

Per Serving: Net Carbs: 5.5g; Calories: 78; Total Fat: 2.8g; Saturated Fat: 1.2g
Protein: 6.8g; Carbs: 7.4g; Fiber: 1.9g; Sugar: 3.6g; Fat 35% / Protein 35% / Carbs 30%

DAY-20 DINNER

Zucchini Cheese Gratin

Serves: 9 / Preparation time: 10 minutes / Cooking time: 50 minutes

4 cups raw zucchini, sliced

1/2 cup heavy whipping cream

1 1/2 cups pepper jack cheese, shredded

1 onion, sliced

1/2 tsp garlic powder

2 tbsp butter

Pepper

Salt

- Preheat the oven to 190 C/ 375 F.

- Spray oven safe pan with cooking spray.

- Add 1/3 sliced onion and zucchini in pan and season with pepper and salt.

- Sprinkle 1/2 cup cheese over sliced onion and zucchini.

- In a microwave safe dish, combine together heavy whipping cream, butter, and garlic powder.

- Microwave for 1 minute or until butter is melted.

- Pour heavy cream mixture over sliced zucchini and onion.

- Bake in preheated oven for 45 minutes.

- Serve and enjoy.

Per Serving: Net Carbs: 3g; Calories: 126; Total Fat: 10.5g; Saturated Fat: 6.5g
Protein: 4.9g; Carbs: 3.8g; Fiber: 0.8g; Sugar: 1.4g; Fat 75% / Protein 15% / Carbs 10%

DAY-21 BREAKFAST

Creamy Egg Scrambled

Serves: 3 / Preparation time: 10 minutes / Cooking time: 15 minutes

5 eggs

3 oz cream cheese

1/3 cup whipping cream

¼ cup onion, chopped

2 tbsp butter

1 tbsp parsley, chopped

Pepper

Salt

- Melt butter in a large pan over low heat.
- Add onion to the pan and sauté until softened.
- Add cream cheese and cream and stir until cream cheese melted.
- In a bowl, whisk eggs with pepper and salt.
- Pour egg mixture into the pan and stir until eggs are set.
- Garnish with parsley and serve.

Per Serving: Net Carbs: 2.4g; Calories: 315 Total Fat: 29g; Saturated Fat: 15.9g
Protein: 11.9g; Carbs: 2.7g; Fiber: 0.3g; Sugar: 1.1g; Fat 82% / Protein 15% / Carbs 3%

DAY-21 LUNCH

Easy Chicken Fajitas

Serves: 6 / Preparation time: 10 minutes / Cooking time: 10 minutes

4 chicken breasts, skinless and boneless

1/2 cup onion, sliced

1/2 cup bell pepper, sliced

1/2 cup water

1 packet fajita seasoning

- Add all ingredients into the instant pot and stir well.

- Seal pot with lid and cook on high pressure for 10 minutes.

- Release pressure using quick release method than open the lid.

- Shred the chicken using fork.

- Serve and enjoy.

Per Serving: Net Carbs: 1.4g; Calories: 192; Total Fat: 7.2g; Saturated Fat: 2g
Protein: 28.4g; Carbs: 1.7g; Fiber: 0.3g; Sugar: 0.9g; Fat 35% / Protein 61% / Carbs 4%

DAY-21 DINNER

Zucchini Noodles

Serves: 2 / Preparation time: 10 minutes / Cooking time: 10 minutes

1 zucchini, spiralized into noodles

1 tbsp butter

1/2 cup water

2/3 cup cheddar cheese, shredded

2 tbsp almond milk

1 tsp salt

- Add noodles, salt, and water in a saucepan and bring to boil.
- Boil noodles until soft and water are completely absorbed.
- Reduce heat to low and add cheese, almond milk, and butter. Stir well to combine.
- Serve and enjoy.

Per Serving: Net Carbs: 3.2g; Calories: 253; Total Fat: 22g; Saturated Fat: 14.8g
Protein: 11g; Carbs: 4.6g; Fiber: 1.4g; Sugar: 2.4g; Fat 78% / Protein 17% / Carbs 5%

DAY-22 BREAKFAST

Cauliflower Cheese Bread

Serves: 10 / Preparation time: 10 minutes / Cooking time: 45 minutes

1 medium cauliflower head, grated

1 tsp basil

1 cup cheddar cheese, divided

2 large eggs

3/4 cup yogurt

1/2 cup parmesan cheese

1 tbsp rosemary

1/2 tsp thyme

1 tsp oregano

1/4 tsp pepper

1/2 tsp salt

- Preheat the oven to 204 C/ 400 F.
- Add all ingredients into the mixing bowl and mix until well combined.
- Pour batter on cookie sheet and line with parchment paper until evenly spread.
- Bake in preheated oven for 40-45 minutes.
- Cut bread into the pieces and serve.

Per Serving: Net Carbs: 3.4g; Calories: 106 Total Fat: 6.2g; Saturated Fat: 3.6g
Protein: 7.8g; Carbs: 5.1g; Fiber: 1.7g; Sugar: 2.8g; Fat 55% / Protein 31% / Carbs 14%

DAY-22 LUNCH

Mayo Cabbage Coleslaw

Serves: 4 / Preparation time: 10 minutes / Cooking time: 30 minutes

3 cups cabbage, shredded

1 tsp dried dill

1 tbsp red wine vinegar

1/3 cup mayonnaise

5 drops liquid stevia

1/2 tsp onion powder

1 tsp salt

- In a large bowl, mix together mayonnaise, stevia, onion powder, dill, vinegar, and salt.

- Add shredded cabbage to the bowl and stir well to combine. Place in refrigerator for 30 minutes.

- Serve and enjoy.

Per Serving: Net Carbs: 2.1g; Calories: 136; Total Fat: 13.4g; Saturated Fat: 2g
Protein: 0.8g; Carbs: 3.5g; Fiber: 1.4g; Sugar: 1.8g; Fat 90% / Protein 3% / Carbs 7%

DAY-22 DINNER

Cauliflower Cheese Gratin

Serves: 4 / Preparation time: 10 minutes / Cooking time: 25 minutes

4 cups cauliflower florets

1/3 cup heavy whipping cream

4 tbsp butter

6 pepper jack cheese slices

Pepper

Salt

- Add cauliflower florets, pepper, salt, heavy whipping cream and butter in oven safe dish.

- Place dish in oven and microwave for 25 minutes.

- Slightly mash the cauliflower florets using back of spoon.

- Place cheese slices over cauliflower mixture and microwave for 2 minutes or until cheese melted.

- Serve and enjoy.

Per Serving: Net Carbs: 3.1g; Calories: 281; Total Fat: 24.3g; Saturated Fat: 14.9g
Protein: 9.8g; Carbs: 5.6g; Fiber: 2.5g; Sugar: 2.4g; Fat 79% / Protein 15% / Carbs 6%

DAY-23 BREAKFAST

Herb Cauliflower Bread

Serves: 10 / Preparation time: 10 minutes / Cooking time: 30 minutes

2 eggs

1/4 tsp red chili flakes, crushed

2 tsp fresh parsley, chopped

1/2 cup parmesan cheese, grated

1/2 tsp oregano, dried

2 garlic cloves, minced

1 large cauliflower head, grated

3 cups mozzarella cheese, shredded and divided

1/4 tsp pepper

1/2 tsp salt

- Preheat the oven to 218 C/ 425 F.

- Line baking tray with parchment paper.

- In a mixing bowl, combine together cauliflower, 1 cup mozzarella cheese, oregano, garlic, parmesan cheese, eggs, pepper, and salt.

- Place dough on baking tray and pat into a crust.

- Bake in preheated oven for 25 minutes.

- Sprinkle remaining cheese, parsley, and red chili flakes and bake for 5 minutes more or until cheese are melted.

- Cut into slices and serve.

Per Serving: Net Carbs: 2.9g; Calories: 89 Total Fat: 4.3g; Saturated Fat: 2.4g
Protein: 7.6g; Carbs: 5.1g; Fiber: 2.2g; Sugar: 2.1g; Fat 47% / Protein 37% / Carbs 16%

DAY-23 LUNCH

Cabbage Dill Cucumber Salad

Serves: 8 / Preparation time: 10 minutes / Cooking time: 10 minutes

1/2 head cabbage, shredded

2 tbsp green onions, chopped

2 tbsp fresh dill, chopped

2 cucumbers, sliced

3 tbsp olive oil

1/2 lemon juice

Pepper

Salt

- Add shredded cabbage and 1 tsp salt into the bowl and set aside to release juices.
- Add remaining ingredients to the cabbage bowl and stir well.
- Serve and enjoy.

Per Serving: Net Carbs: 4.2g; Calories: 71; Total Fat: 5.4g; Saturated Fat: 0.8g
Protein: 1.3g; Carbs: 5.9g; Fiber: 1.7g; Sugar: 2.8g; Fat 69% / Protein 8% / Carbs 23%

DAY-23 DINNER

Cheese Cauliflower Rice

Serves: 6 / Preparation time: 10 minutes / Cooking time: 5 minutes

1 cauliflower head, cut into florets

1/4 tsp garlic powder

2 oz cream cheese

2.5 oz cheddar cheese, shredded

1/4 tsp pepper

1/4 tsp salt

- Add cauliflower florets into the food processor and process until it looks like rice.
- Transfer cauliflower rice to the baking dish and microwave for 5 minutes.
- Add cream cheese and cheddar cheese and stir until melted.
- Add garlic powder, pepper, and salt and stir well.
- Serve and enjoy.

Per Serving: Net Carbs: 1.8g; Calories: 92; Total Fat: 7.3g; Saturated Fat: 4.6g
Protein: 4.6g; Carbs: 2.9g; Fiber: 1.1g; Sugar: 1.2g; Fat 72% / Protein 20% / Carbs 8%

DAY-24 BREAKFAST

Vanilla protein Muffins

Serves: 6 / Preparation time: 5 minutes / Cooking time: 25 minutes

4 eggs

1 scoop whey protein powder

1 tsp vanilla

2 tbsp butter

4 oz cream cheese

- Spray muffin tray with cooking spray and set aside.

- In a bowl, melt cream cheese and butter.

- Add eggs, vanilla, and whey protein in a bowl and mix until well combined.

- Pour batter into the prepared muffin tray and bake at 176 C/ 350 F for 25 minutes.

- Serve and enjoy.

Per Serving: Net Carbs: 1.4g; Calories: 164 Total Fat: 13.7g; Saturated Fat: 7.6g
Protein: 8.9g; Carbs: 1.4g; Fiber: 0g; Sugar: 0.5g; Fat 75% / Protein 21% / Carbs 4%

DAY-24 LUNCH

Healthy Coconut Spinach Soup

Serves: 4 / Preparation time: 105 minutes / Cooking time: 15 minutes

2 cups baby spinach, wash and pat dry

2 cups vegetable broth

1/2 tsp ginger, grated

1/2 onion, diced

2 cups cauliflower florets

1 tbsp olive oil

1 tbsp coconut cream

1 cup fresh parsley, chopped

- Heat olive oil in a saucepan over medium heat.

- Add onion and sauté until translucent. Add cauliflower and cook until softened.

- Add broth and stir well. Cover saucepan and bring to boil.

- Once vegetable is soften than add spinach, coconut cream, ginger, and parsley. Stir until spinach wilted.

- Remove from heat and puree the soup using immersion blender until smooth.

- Serve and enjoy.

Per Serving: Net Carbs: 3.8g; Calories: 85; Total Fat: 5.3g; Saturated Fat: 1.5g
Protein: 4.6g; Carbs: 6.3g; Fiber: 2.5g; Sugar: 2.5g; Fat 58% / Protein 23% / Carbs 19%

DAY-24 DINNER

Baked Broccoli

Serves: 4 / Preparation time: 10 minutes / Cooking time: 10 minutes

1 broccoli stalk, cut into florets

1/4 cup parmesan cheese, grated

1/2 cup heavy cream

2 garlic cloves, minced

1/2 cup gruyere, shredded

1/2 cup mozzarella cheese, shredded

1 tbsp butter

Pepper

Salt

- Preheat the oven to 190 C/ 375 F.

- Melt butter in an oven-safe pan over medium-high heat.

- Add broccoli florets in a pan and season with pepper and salt.

- Cook broccoli florets for 5 minutes or until tender. Add garlic and stir for 1 minute.

- Add heavy cream on top of broccoli then top with parmesan, gruyere, and mozzarella cheese.

- Place pan in preheated oven and bake broccoli for 10 minutes.

- Serve and enjoy.

Per Serving: Net Carbs: 2g; Calories: 303; Total Fat: 22.5g; Saturated Fat: 14.2g
Protein: 18.3g; Carbs: 2.6g; Fiber: 0.6g; Sugar: 0.5g; Fat 69% / Protein 26% / Carbs 5%

DAY-25 BREAKFAST

Coconut Kale Muffins

Serves: 8 / Preparation time: 10 minutes / Cooking time: 30 minutes

6 eggs

1/2 cup coconut milk

1 cup kale, chopped

1/4 cup chives, chopped

Pepper

Salt

- Preheat the oven to 176 C/ 350 F.

- Spray muffin tray with cooking spray and set aside.

- Add all ingredients into the bowl and whisk well to combined.

- Pour mixture into the prepared muffin tray and bake in preheated oven for 30 minutes.

- Serve and enjoy.

Per Serving: Net Carbs: 1.5g; Calories: 86 Total Fat: 6.9g; Saturated Fat: 4.2g
Protein: 4.8g; Carbs: 2g; Fiber: 0.5g; Sugar: 0.8g; Fat 72% / Protein 22% / Carbs 6%

DAY-25 LUNCH

Garlic Herb Baked Mushrooms

Serves: 6 / Preparation time: 10 minutes / Cooking time: 20 minutes

1 lb button mushrooms, scrubbed and stems trimmed

2 tbsp olive oil

4 tbsp balsamic vinegar

1/4 tsp black pepper

1/2 tsp dried basil

1/2 tsp dried oregano

3 garlic cloves, crushed

1 tsp sea salt

- Preheat the oven to 215 C/ 425 F.

- Spray a baking tray with cooking spray and set aside.

- In a mixing bowl, mix together vinegar, basil, oregano, garlic, olive oil, pepper, and salt.

- Stir in mushrooms and let sit for 15 minutes.

- Spread mushrooms onto the prepared baking tray and bake in preheated oven for 15-20 minutes.

- Serve and enjoy.

Per Serving: Net Carbs: 2.3g; Calories: 61; Total Fat: 4.9g; Saturated Fat: 0.7g
Protein: 2.5g; Carbs: 3.2g; Fiber: 0.9g; Sugar: 1.4g; Fat 71% / Protein 14% / Carbs 15%

DAY-25 DINNER

Parmesan Spinach Pie

Serves: 6 / Preparation time: 10 minutes / Cooking time: 60 minutes

4 eggs

1/2 cup heavy cream

16 oz cottage cheese

2 tbsp parmesan cheese, grated

1 tsp garlic, minced

8 oz mushrooms, sliced

10 oz fresh spinach

1/2 cup mozzarella cheese, shredded

1/4 tsp nutmeg

1/2 tsp pepper

2 tsp olive oil

1 tsp salt

- Preheat the oven to 176 C/ 350 F.
- Heat oil in a pan over medium heat.
- Add mushrooms and garlic in a pan and sauté until tender.
- Add spinach, nutmeg, pepper, and salt and cook until spinach is wilted.
- Drain spinach and mushrooms mixture.
- Sprinkle parmesan cheese into the 9" pie dish.
- In a bowl, whisk together eggs, cottage cheese, and cream and stir well.
- Add mushroom and spinach mixture and stir well.
- Pour mushroom and spinach mixture into a pie dish and bake in preheated oven for 50 minutes.
- Slice and serve.

Per Serving: Net Carbs: 5.1g; Calories: 198; Total Fat: 11.1g; Saturated Fat: 5.2g
Protein: 18.6g; Carbs: 6.6g; Fiber: 1.5g; Sugar: 1.4g; Fat 51% / Protein 38% / Carbs 11%

DAY-26 BREAKFAST

Spicy & Creamy Egg Scrambled

Serves: 2 / Preparation time: 10 minutes / Cooking time: 10 minutes

4 eggs

2 tbsp cilantro, chopped

1/3 cup heavy cream

1 tomato, diced

1 Serrano chili pepper, chopped

2 tbsp scallions, sliced

1/4 tsp black pepper

3 tbsp butter

1/2 tsp salt

- Melt butter in a pan over medium heat.

- Add tomato and chili pepper and sauté for 2 minutes.

- In a bowl, whisk together eggs, cilantro, cream, pepper, and salt.

- Pour egg mixture into the pan and stir until egg is set.

- Top with scallions and serve.

Per Serving: Net Carbs: 3g; Calories: 358 Total Fat: 33.5g; Saturated Fat: 18.3g
Protein: 12.1g; Carbs: 3.6g; Fiber: 0.6g; Sugar: 1.7g; Fat 84% / Protein 13% / Carbs 3%

DAY-26 LUNCH

Creamy Cauliflower Broccoli Mashed

Serves: 4 / Preparation time: 10 minutes / Cooking time: 10 minutes

2 cups cauliflower florets

1 tbsp olive oil

2 cups broccoli florets

3 garlic cloves, peeled

1/2 tsp pepper

1/2 tsp salt

- Heat olive oil in a pan over medium heat.
- Add cauliflower, broccoli, and salt in a pan and sauté until softened.
- Transfer vegetables and garlic to the food processor and process until smooth.
- Season with pepper and salt.
- Serve and enjoy.

Per Serving: Net Carbs: 4g; Calories: 62; Total Fat: 3.7g; Saturated Fat: 0.5g
Protein: 2.4g; Carbs: 6.6g; Fiber: 2.6g; Sugar: 2g; Fat 56% / Protein 17% / Carbs 27%

DAY-26 DINNER

Almond Jalapeno Pizza

Serves: 4 / Preparation time: 10 minutes / Cooking time: 20 minutes

1/3 cup almond flour

1/4 tsp garlic powder

1 egg, beaten

3/4 cup mozzarella cheese, shredded

1 cup cheddar cheese, shredded

2 jalapeno pepper, sliced

2 oz cream cheese

- Preheat the oven to 176 C/ 350 F.
- In a small bowl, add mozzarella cheese and cream cheese. Microwave on high for 20 seconds or until melted.
- Add remaining ingredients to the melted cheese and stir well.
- Spray 10" pan with cooking spray and spread the dough out evenly.
- Bake in preheated oven for 10 minutes.
- Top with jalapenos and cheese and cook for 10 minutes more.
- Serve and enjoy.

Per Serving: Net Carbs: 1.6g; Calories: 210; Total Fat: 17.5g; Saturated Fat: 10.1g
Protein: 11.6g; Carbs: 2.1g; Fiber: 0.5g; Sugar: 0.6g; Fat 75% / Protein 22% / Carbs 3%

DAY-27 BREAKFAST

Cinnamon Cream Egg Scrambled

Serves: 2 / Preparation time: 5 minutes / Cooking time: 10 minutes

4 eggs

1/4 tsp ground cinnamon

2 tbsp cream

1 tbsp butter

- In a bowl, whisk together cream and eggs until smooth.

- Melt butter in a pan over medium heat.

- Add egg mixture in a pan and cook until egg is set.

- Top with cinnamon and serve.

Per Serving: Net Carbs: 1.1g; Calories: 185 Total Fat: 15.2g; Saturated Fat: 6.8g
Protein: 11.2g; Carbs: 1.3g; Fiber: 0.2g; Sugar: 0.9g; Fat 73% / Protein 24% / Carbs 3%

DAY-27 LUNCH

Paprika Egg Cucumber Salad

Serves: 4 / Preparation time: 10 minutes / Cooking time: 5 minutes

6 hard-boiled eggs

1 avocado, peel and cubed

1 medium cucumber, peeled and chopped

1/2 tsp paprika

1/4 cup mayonnaise

- Peel the eggs and cut into pieces.
- Add all ingredients into the mixing bowl and toss well to combined.
- Serve and enjoy.

Per Serving: Net Carbs: 2.9g; Calories: 211; Total Fat: 17.9g; Saturated Fat: 3.8g
Protein: 9.1g; Carbs: 4.1g; Fiber: 1.2g; Sugar: 1.8g; Fat 76% / Protein 18% / Carbs 6%

DAY-27 DINNER

Spinach Casserole

Serves: 6 / Preparation time: 10 minutes / Cooking time: 35 minutes

2 eggs

1 1/4 cup cheddar cheese, shredded

1/2 red pepper, chopped

2 cups frozen spinach, thawed and drained

1 1/2 cups egg whites

1/2 green pepper, chopped

1/2 onion, chopped

1 cup mushrooms, sliced

Pepper

Salt

- Preheat the oven to 176 C/ 375 F.
- Spray casserole dish with cooking spray and set aside.
- Heat pan over medium-high heat.
- Add chopped vegetables except spinach to the pan and sauté for few minutes until vegetables are soft.
- Add vegetables to the bottom of casserole dish and spread the vegetables to the dish.
- Add spinach to the vegetables and spread well.
- Whisk eggs and egg whites in a small bowl and season with pepper and salt.
- Pour egg mixture over the vegetables.
- Sprinkle with shredded cheese.
- Bake in preheated oven for 35 minutes.
- Serve and enjoy.

Per Serving: Net Carbs: 2.8g; Calories: 161; Total Fat: 9.5g; Saturated Fat: 5.4g
Protein: 15.3g; Carbs: 3.7g; Fiber: 0.9g; Sugar: 2g; Fat 54% / Protein 39% / Carbs 7%

DAY-28 BREAKFAST

Flavorful Cheese Quiche

Serves: 8 / Preparation time: 5 minutes / Cooking time: 45 minutes

12 eggs

8 oz cheddar cheese, grated

3/4 cup butter

4 oz cream cheese, softened

Pepper

Salt

- Add half cup cheese to the 10-inch pie pan.

- Add eggs, cream cheese, and butter into the blender and blend until well combined.

- Pour egg mixture over cheese in pie pan. Season with pepper and salt.

- Sprinkle remaining cheese on top of egg mixture and bake at 162 C/ 325 F for 45 minutes.

- Serve and enjoy.

Per Serving: Net Carbs: 1.3g; Calories: 411 Total Fat: 38.2g; Saturated Fat: 22.1g
Protein: 16.6g; Carbs: 1.3g; Fiber: 0g; Sugar: 0.7g; Fat 83% / Protein 16% / Carbs 1%

DAY-28 LUNCH

Easy Caesar Salad

Serves: 8 / Preparation time: 10 minutes / Cooking time: 5 minutes

8 cups romaine lettuce, chopped

2 tbsp fresh lemon juice

1/4 cup olive oil

1/4 cup parmesan cheese, grated

1/4 tsp garlic powder

1 tbsp mayonnaise

1/4 tsp pepper

1/8 tsp salt

- In a large bowl, combine together olive oil, garlic powder, mayonnaise, and lemon juice.
- Add lettuce and cheese in a bowl. Season with pepper and salt.
- Cover bowl and place in refrigerator for 1 hour.
- Toss well and serve.

Per Serving: Net Carbs: 1.9g; Calories: 145; Total Fat: 11.5g; Saturated Fat: 4g
Protein: 6.3g; Carbs: 2.3g; Fiber: 0.4g; Sugar: 0.8g; Fat 74% / Protein 19% / Carbs 7%

DAY-28 DINNER

Cheese Chicken Casserole

Serves: 8 / Preparation time: 10 minutes / Cooking time: 40 minutes

2 lbs cooked chicken, shredded

6 oz cream cheese, softened

4 oz butter, melted

6 oz ham, cut into small pieces

5 oz Swiss cheese

1 oz fresh lemon juice

1 tbsp Dijon mustard

½ tsp salt

- Preheat the oven to 176 C/ 350 F.
- Place chicken in the bottom of baking dish then layer ham pieces on top.
- Add butter, lemon juice, mustard, cream cheese, and salt into the blender and blend until a thick sauce.
- Spread sauce over top of chicken and ham mixture in the baking dish.
- Arrange Swiss cheese slices on top of sauce.
- Bake in preheated oven for 40 minutes.
- Serve and enjoy.

Per Serving: Net Carbs: 2.1g; Calories: 451; Total Fat: 29.2g; Saturated Fat: 16.7g
Protein: 43g; Carbs: 2.5g; Fiber: 0.4g; Sugar: 0.4g; Fat 59% / Protein 39% / Carbs 2%

DAY-29 BREAKFAST

Tasty Cauliflower Frittata

Serves: 1 / Preparation time: 10 minutes / Cooking time: 15 minutes

1 egg

1/2 tbsp onion, diced

5 tbsp cauliflower rice

1 tbsp olive oil

1/4 tsp turmeric

1/8 tsp black pepper

Salt

- Add all ingredients except oil into the bowl and mix well to combine.
- Heat oil in a pan over medium heat.
- Using spoon scoop the mixture and pour into the hot pan and cook for 3-4 minutes or until lightly golden brown.
- Serve and enjoy.

Per Serving: Net Carbs: 1.9g; Calories: 195 Total Fat: 18.5g; Saturated Fat: 3.4g
Protein: 6.3g; Carbs: 3g; Fiber: 1.1g; Sugar: 1.3g; Fat 85% / Protein 12% / Carbs 3%

DAY-29 LUNCH

Flavors Squash Soup

Serves: 8 / Preparation time: 10 minutes / Cooking time: 35 minutes

1 lb butternut squash, peeled and diced

5 tbsp olive oil, divided

1/2 cup heavy cream

1 bay leaf

4 cups vegetable broth

3 garlic cloves, minced

1 tsp sea salt

- Heat 1 tablespoon of olive oil in a saucepan over medium heat.
- Add butternut squash, salt, and garlic and sauté until lightly golden brown.
- Add broth, remaining oil, and bay leaves in a saucepan. Bring to boil.
- Simmer for 30 minutes or until squash cooked completely.
- Discard bay leaves from soup.
- Puree the soup using immersion blender until smooth and creamy.
- Add heavy cream and stir well.
- Serve and enjoy.

Per Serving: Net Carbs: 6.3g; Calories: 171; Total Fat: 14.5g; Saturated Fat: 5g
Protein: 3.1g; Carbs: 7.5g; Fiber: 1.2g; Sugar: 1.6g; Fat 77% / Protein 8% / Carbs 15%

DAY-29 DINNER

Spicy Chicken Curry

Serves: 6 / Preparation time: 10 minutes / Cooking time: 20 minutes

1 ½ lbs chicken thighs, skinless, boneless, and cut into pieces

1 cup tomatoes, chopped

1 tbsp jalapeno pepper, minced

2 tbsp ginger, diced

2 tbsp olive oil

¼ cup fresh cilantro, chopped

2 tbsp fresh lemon juice

2 tsp cayenne

1 tsp garam masala

2 tsp turmeric

- Heat olive oil in a pan over medium heat.
- Add jalapenos and ginger to the pan and sauté for 2-3 minutes.
- Add chicken and sear chicken from both the sides. Add tomatoes and stir well.
- Add all spices and stir well and cook until chicken is completely cooked and tomatoes soften.
- Add lemon juice and stir well.
- Garnish with chopped cilantro and serve.

Per Serving: Net Carbs: 2.4g; Calories: 273; Total Fat: 13.5g; Saturated Fat: 3.1g
Protein: 33.4g; Carbs: 3.4g; Fiber: 1g; Sugar: 1.1g; Fat 46% / Protein 50% / Carbs 4%

DAY-30 BREAKFAST

Mushroom Asparagus Frittata

Serves: 4 / Preparation time: 10 minutes / Cooking time: 15 minutes

6 eggs

3 mushrooms, sliced

10 asparagus, chopped

1/4 cup half and half

2 tsp butter

1 cup mozzarella cheese, shredded

1 tsp black pepper

1 tsp salt

- Melt butter in oven safe pan over medium heat.
- Add mushrooms in a pan and sauté for 5 minutes.
- Add asparagus and sauté for 2 minutes.
- Meanwhile, in a bowl, whisk together eggs, half and half, pepper, and salt and pour over asparagus. Cook over medium heat until set.
- Sprinkle cheese on top and transfer pan to the oven and cook for 5 minutes.
- Cut into pieces and serve.

Per Serving: Net Carbs: 2.5g; Calories: 161 Total Fat: 11.6g; Saturated Fat: 5.1g
Protein: 11.9g; Carbs: 3.4g; Fiber: 0.9g; Sugar: 1.3g; Fat 65% / Protein 30% / Carbs 5%

DAY-30 LUNCH

Simple Broccoli Omelet

Serves: 2 / Preparation time: 10 minutes / Cooking time: 10 minutes

4 eggs

1 tbsp olive oil

1 cup broccoli, chopped and cooked

1 tbsp fresh parsley, chopped

1/4 tsp pepper

1/2 tsp salt

- In a bowl, whisk eggs with pepper, and salt.
- Heat olive oil in a pan over medium heat.
- Add broccoli and eggs mixture into the pan and cook until set.
- Turn omelet to other side and cook until lightly golden brown.
- Garnish with chopped parsley.
- Serve and enjoy.

Per Serving: Net Carbs: 2.7g; Calories: 203; Total Fat: 15.9g; Saturated Fat: 3.7g
Protein: 12.4g; Carbs: 4g; Fiber: 1.3g; Sugar: 1.5g; Fat 71% / Protein 25% / Carbs 4%

DAY-30 DINNER

Meatloaf

Serves: 8 / Preparation time: 10 minutes / Cooking time: 40 minutes

2 eggs

1/2 cup parmesan cheese, grated

1/2 cup marinara sauce, sugar free

1 cup cottage cheese

1 lb mozzarella cheese, cut into cubes

2 lbs ground turkey

2 tsp Italian seasoning

1/4 cup basil pesto

1 tsp salt

- Preheat the oven to 204 C/ 400 F.

- Spray casserole dish with cooking spray and set aside.

- Add all ingredients into the mixing bowl and mix until well combined.

- Transfer bowl mixture to the prepared casserole dish and bake in preheated oven for 40 minutes.

- Serve and enjoy.

Per Serving: Net Carbs: 3.1g; Calories: 327; Total Fat: 17.7g; Saturated Fat: 4.8g
Protein: 40.6g; Carbs: 3.5g; Fiber: 0.4g; Sugar: 1.7g; Fat 49% / Protein 48% / Carbs 3%

References and resources

For those who want to spend more time researching the Ketogenic Diet, there are some great references and resources that you can rely on to learn more about this amazing eating style that has changed millions of lives.

Below are some of the best sources for further education on this topic:

The Keto Diet: The Complete Guide to a High-Fat Diet, with More Than 125 Delectable Recipes and 5 Meal Plans to Shed Weight, Heal Your Body, and Regain Confidence

This book is one of the best in the keto series because it truly provides high definition explanations regarding the Ketogenic Diet and is also backed by scientific evidence. It is usually one of the favorite books for people who are only just starting their keto journey.

Ketogenic Diet : The Step by Step Guide For Beginners: Ketogenic Diet for Beginners : Optimal Path for Weight Loss

This is perhaps a more simplified version of the previous book, but it is also great because it explains the Ketogenic Diet with more efficiency. This is a great choice for people who really don't want to turn this whole experience into a science, but would rather have a quick read through and immediately get on with it.

Simply Keto: A Practical Approach to Health & Weight Loss, with 100+ Easy Low-Carb Recipes

This book has quickly become known as one of the most inspirational books about the Ketogenic Diet. It truly focuses on the most difficult part of this diet which are the early stages when people are still trying to get used to the concept and to let go of their previous ways of eating and living. This is a great book for people who know that it will take them a while to make changes to their lifestyle, and who really need a source of support to make sure that they will definitely reach the stage of ketosis and actually continue with it.

THE "DIRTY DOZEN" AND "CLEAN 15"

The Environmental Working Group (EWG) publishes annual lists of produce containing the highest and lowest levels of pesticide residue. The lists are based on analyzing data from the USDA Pesticide Data Program report.

The EWG found that a majority (70%) of the 48 different kinds of produce tested contained some residue of at least one type of pesticide. Overall they found 178 different kinds of pesticides. This pesticide residue can remain on produce despite washing and peeling. Every kind of pesticide is toxic for people and ingesting them can cause damage to the immune system, reproductive system, nervous system, cancer, and more. Pregnant women may harm the health and development of the unborn baby as a result of consuming pesticide residue.

Keep these facts in mind when you are selecting produce and deciding whether to buy organic.

THE DIRTY DOZEN

- Celery
- Pears
- Spinach
- Strawberries
- Apples
- Nectarines
- Peaches
- Grapes
- Cherries
- Sweet bell peppers
- Tomatoes
- Potatoes

THE CLEAN 15

- Eggplant
- Cauliflower
- Sweet corn
- Pineapples
- Avocados
- Onions
- Cabbage
- Frozen sweet peas
- Asparagus
- Papayas
- Mangoes
- Honeydew
- Cantaloupe
- Kiwi
- Grapefruit

Measurement Conversion Tables

Volume Equivalents (Dry)

US Standard	Metric (Approx.)
¼ teaspoon	1 ml
½ teaspoon	2 ml
1 teaspoon	5 ml
1 tablespoon	15 ml
¼ cup	59 ml
½ cup	118 ml
1 cup	235 ml

Weight Equivalents

US Standard	Metric (Approx.)
½ ounce	15 g
1 ounce	30 g
2 ounces	60 g
4 ounces	115 g
8 ounces	225 g
12 ounces	340 g
16 oz or 1 lb	455 g

Volume Equivalents (Liquid)

US Standard	US Standard (ounces)	Metric (Approx.)
2 tablespoons	1 fl oz	30 ml
¼ cup	2 fl oz	60 ml
½ cup	4 fl oz	120 ml
1 cup	8 fl oz	240 ml
1 ½ cups	12 fl oz	355 ml
2 cups or 1 pint	16 fl oz	475 ml
4 cups or 1 quart	32 fl oz	1 L
1 gallon	128 fl oz	4 L

Oven Temperatures

Fahrenheit (F)	Celsius (C) (Approx)
250°F	120°C
300°F	150°C
325°F	165°C
350°F	180°C
375°F	190°C
400°F	200°C
425°F	220°C
450°F	230°C

Final Note from the Author

The Ketogenic Diet is not the only way to live a healthy lifestyle, but it is certainly one of the rare options where there is actual scientific research that successfully backs the use of this diet to live a healthier life. All change is difficult in the beginning, and some people find it easier to switch to new ways of living their life and eating than others. It is also understandable that some people will revert to their old ways of eating and perhaps not exercising throughout the process, which is also not something that happens rarely. The most important thing to remember is that we all handle life differently, and we all have things which make our lives both easy and difficult. Having said that, you need to remember that the most important thing is that you must never give up. There is no one in the world who can just wake up one day and suddenly be a different person, however, it is persistence that will truly help you to live a better life and to be there longer for your family.

If you know that you are one of these people who will need some extra time before they are fully able to become users of the Ketogenic Diet, there are a number of ways that you can help yourself throughout this journey. Many people think that it is a great idea to prepare a calendar or a planner to help them throughout the process. They use these things to mark the days when they were successful in their journey and when they were not. They also use a plan to monitor the amount of water that they have drunk throughout the day. They use the planner to plan the meals throughout the week and the grocery shopping that also needs to be done in return. They use the planners for inspirational messages, and much more. Whatever it is that will motivate you to live a better life is a good idea. There is no reason to think that a transition to a different diet needs to be difficult in any way. You can also join support groups, or invite friends and family to help you on this journey.

Once you start the Ketogenic Diet, you will quickly realize that it will only take a few days before you are fully hooked onto this lifestyle. After a few months, you will no longer wish to return to your old ways of eating and living, which were making your body unhealthy and feeling horrible.

Luckily, Ketogenic Diet recipes are very easy to prepare and plan, and you can also easily adapt them to your own tastes and your own favorite ingredients. You will quickly notice how much easier life is when you have the correct plan for all of your meals throughout the week. You will not be tempted to snack on nutritionally poor products. Instead, you will have healthy snacks that will actually refresh your body instead of making it feel worse and causing insulin jumps and drops that are responsible for the afternoon naps that so many people feel that they absolutely must take.

Stick to the plan, read as much as you possible can about the Ketogenic Diet and make sure that you understand the importance of what it is that you are about to achieve with this new way of living. You will soon realize that this was the best decision that you have ever made for your body and your overall health.

Alphabetical Recipe Index

Almond Blueberry Muffins	45
Almond Chicken Salad	63
Almond Jalapeno Pizza	110
Almond Pumpkin Pancake	86
Avocado Bacon Soup	72
Bacon Avocado Chicken Salad	37
Bacon Avocado Quiche	80
Bacon Cheese Bread	68
Baked Broccoli	103
Blueberry Almond Coconut Flour Casserole	89
Cabbage Dill Cucumber Salad	99
Cauliflower Cheese Bread	95
Cauliflower Cheese Casserole	34
Cauliflower Cheese Casserole	58
Cauliflower Cheese Gratin	97
Cheddar Broccoli Bread	48
Cheese Broccoli Soup	61
Cheese Cauliflower Rice	100
Cheese Chicken Casserole	117
Chicken Basil Salad	43
Chili Garlic Shrimp	69
Cilantro Shrimp Avocado Salad	78
Cinnamon Cream Egg Scrambled	111
Coconut Chia Pudding	71
Coconut Kale Muffins	104
Coconut Waffles	59
Creamy Cauliflower Broccoli Mashed	109
Creamy Cheesy Cauliflower Mash	33
Creamy Egg Salad	40
Creamy Egg Scrambled	92
Cucumber Tuna Salad	66
Curried Chicken Salad	60
Delicious Breakfast Cookies	65

Delicious Mexican Frittata	29
Delicious Ranch Chicken	67
Delicious Ricotta Omelet	52
Delicious Zucchini Soup	90
Easy Breakfast Bowl	39
Easy Cabbage Noodles	57
Easy Caesar Salad	116
Easy Chicken Fajitas	93
Easy Egg Loaf	62
Egg Breakfast Casserole	42
Flavorful Cheese Quiche	115
Flavorful Chicken Piccata	31
Flavorful Citrusy Shrimp	53
Flavorful Tuna Salad	49
Flavors Squash Soup	119
Garlic Herb Baked Mushrooms	105
Garlic Onion Pork Tenderloin	76
Healthy Coconut Porridge	77
Healthy Coconut Spinach Soup	102
Healthy Egg Breakfast Muffins	32
Healthy Mediterranean Salad	84
Healthy Spinach Quiche	83
Herb Cauliflower Bread	98
Herb Chicken	88
Italian Pepperoni Avocado Salad	75
Jalapeno Muffins	36
Lemon Garlic Chicken	79
Lemon Parmesan Salmon	73
Mayo Cabbage Coleslaw	96
Mayo Shrimp Cilantro Salad	46
Meatloaf	123
Mushroom Asparagus Frittata	121
Olive Bacon Quiche	55
Paprika Egg Cucumber Salad	112
Parmesan Spinach Pie	106
Perfect Bacon Chicken	38

Perfect Geek Salad	81
Pesto Cheese Salmon	70
Quick Cherry Tomato Frittata	41
Refreshing Creamy Cucumber Salad	87
Shrimp Mushroom Soup	64
Simple Broccoli Omelet	122
Simple Coconut Shrimp	47
Simple Old Bay Seasoned Shrimp	54
Smoked Paprika Chicken	44
Spicy & Creamy Egg Scrambled	108
Spicy Chicken Curry	120
Spinach Bacon Frittata	74
Spinach Casserole	113
Tasty Cauliflower Frittata	118
Tasty Chicken Guacamole Salad	30
Tasty Pumpkin Spiced Soup	85
Tuna Egg Bake	50
Vanilla protein Muffins	101
Zucchini Cheese Casserole	82
Zucchini Cheese Gratin	91
Zucchini Noodles	94

Manufactured by Amazon.ca
Bolton, ON